AQA BUSINESS for GCSE

GROWING AS A BUSINESS

NEIL DENBY

DAVID HAMMAN

DYNAMIC
LEARNING

HODDER
EDUCATION
AN HACHETTE UK COMPANY

Orders: please contact Bookpoint Ltd, 130 Milton Park, Abingdon, Oxon OX14 4SB. Telephone: (44) 01235 827720. Fax: (44) 01235 400454. Lines are open 9.00–5.00, Monday to Saturday, with a 24-hour message answering service. You can also order through our website www.hoddereducation.co.uk.

British Library Cataloguing in Publication Data

A catalogue record for this title is available from the British Library

ISBN: 978 0340 986646

First Published 2009

Impression number   10 9 8 7 6 5 4 3 2

Year   2012

Cover photo © Olga Zorina/iStockphoto.com

Typeset by Phoenix Photosetting, Chatham, Kent.

Illustrations by Oxford Designers and Illustrators.

Printed in Dubai for Hodder Education, an Hachette UK Company, 338 Euston Road, London NW1 3BH

Contents

How to use this book   v
The AQA GCSE Business specification   ix
Acknowledgements   xi

Section 1   Business Organisation

Chapter 1   Introduction to business organisation   2
Chapter 2   Expanding as a business   5
Chapter 3   Choosing the right legal structure   11
Chapter 4   Business aims and objectives   17
Chapter 5   Business location   22

Section 2   Advanced Marketing

Chapter 6   Introduction to advanced marketing   30
Chapter 7   The marketing mix: product   33
Chapter 8   The marketing mix: price   39
Chapter 9   The marketing mix: promotion   44
Chapter 10   The marketing mix: place   50

Section 3   Finance for a Large Business

Chapter 11   Introduction to finance for a large business   58
Chapter 12   Sources of finance for a large business   61
Chapter 13   Profit and loss accounts   67
Chapter 14   Balance sheets   74
Chapter 15   Ratios   81

Section 4   Advanced People in Businesses

Chapter 16   Introduction to advanced people in businesses   90
Chapter 17   Organising a growing business   92
Chapter 18   Recruiting staff   98
Chapter 19   Appraisal and training   105
Chapter 20   Motivation   111

Section 5   Advanced Operations Management

Chapter 21   Introduction to advanced operations management   120
Chapter 22   Production methods   123
Chapter 23   Efficiency and lean production   129
Chapter 24   Benefits and challenges of growth   135
Chapter 25   Maintaining quality assurance in growing businesses 141

Preparing for the controlled assessment   146
Appendix: International Financial Reporting Standards   149
Index   151

How to use this book

This book provides information, exercises and materials to cover the learning required for the second part of the new AQA GCSE Business Studies Full course.

The new qualification has several routes, but all begin with the first unit, 'Setting Up a Business'. This unit is an introduction to setting up and running a business, and looks at the factors that might help the business to succeed, or cause it to fail. It also shows that businesses operate within societies and communities, and that they must therefore take a number of people and their views into account when operating. This is covered in a companion book, *AQA Business for GCSE: Setting up a Business*.

The fact that you are studying this unit, Growing as a Business, means you are working towards the **Full GCSE**. You will study how businesses grow and complete a coursework-style assignment called a Controlled Assessment. The Controlled Assessment is explained on page 146 of this book.

NB This book covers the National Criteria for Business, on which all business GCSE courses are based, so it will be equally useful for GCSE courses other than AQA.

Getting the most out of this book

The book is divided into five sections. The sections reflect the AQA GCSE specification requirements: Business Organisation, Marketing, Finance, People in Businesses and Operations Management. You don't have to study the course in this order: that's up to you and your teacher. Each topic is approached in a more advanced way than it was in the first unit, with the focus on business growth and therefore larger businesses.

Each chapter is designed to be approached in the same way:

● **Read** the 'In the News' section so that you have put the ideas into context, and can think about how they apply to the real world.

● **Read** the text explaining the ideas.

● **Read** 'Core Knowledge' and 'And More' which give the basic information and then further knowledge about the ideas in the chapter.

● **'Have a Go'** at the exercises and activities to see how well you have understood the material. You can come back to the activities at any time if you need to revise the topic for tests or examinations, or you need to refresh your memory for Controlled Assessments.

IN THE NEWS

Each chapter starts with a short news piece, based on recent events or a situation that puts the ideas discussed in the chapter into a real-world context.

This is followed by links to current websites and e-learning materials, so that the story can be followed up or investigated further, or so that additional information can be found.

After the news piece, the key information needed for the chapter is explained.

Summary

- This set of bullet points summarises the most important information contained in the chapter. You could think of this as the absolute minimum that you should learn from the chapter.

Core knowledge

The Core Knowledge then gives the basic knowledge that all students will need regarding this topic.

And more

Following on from the Core Knowledge, And More provides higher level or more in-depth knowledge for students who are aiming at higher grades or just want to improve their knowledge of a particular area.

Did you know...

These boxes are scattered throughout the book. They contain extra information that is either useful or interesting, and which can often help to put the topic into a real-world context.

Have a go!

This section contains a set of activities and exercises that can be carried out in class or at home in study time. Some are designed to be carried out on your own, others with friends or by using web resources.

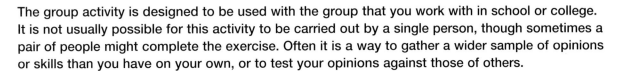

Group activity

The group activity is designed to be used with the group that you work with in school or college. It is not usually possible for this activity to be carried out by a single person, though sometimes a pair of people might complete the exercise. Often it is a way to gather a wider sample of opinions or skills than you have on your own, or to test your opinions against those of others.

Discussion

The discussion may follow on directly from the group activity, perhaps so that you can explore why you did or did not agree, had different views, or had different experiences to share. It will make you think more deeply about the area that you are studying!

Web-based activity

This activity requires access to a computer and an internet connection. It may take you to a specific site or sites, perhaps to see how an idea or knowledge has been put into practice in the real world, or it may ask you to use a search engine to find out more information. There is then a short activity based on what you have found.

Quickfire questions

These questions appear in every chapter. They will test your knowledge of the ideas and information in the chapter. Your teacher might use them to start or end a lesson, as a quiz with the class, or may ask you to complete them on your own. They are usually simple questions with simple answers, designed to check basic knowledge so, for instance, they might ask for definitions and brief explanations.

Hit the spot

> These questions require longer answers, where you can demonstrate your understanding of ideas and information in greater depth.

>> The chevrons (>) show the difficulty levels of the questions. One chevron is used for easier questions, that everyone should be able to do; two chevrons indicate harder questions, where some explanation of the answer is needed. The hardest questions, which may require you to state and justify an opinion, or to weigh up two sides of an argument, have three chevrons.

Cracking the code

Some words in the text are highlighted. These terms are explained under the 'Cracking the Code' heading. In business studies many words have a particular meaning, and it may even be different to how you use the word in normal speech. Cracking the Code will help you to use these words and terms in the correct way.

The AQA GCSE Business specification

The AQA GCSE Business specification is based on the 'story' of a small business enterprise which can then successfully expand. Unit 1 is called Setting up a Business and looks at the business concepts and ideas that are needed to establish a small business – and at how that business might measure its success. Unit 2, Growing as a Business, shows how the business could grow, and the changes that it would have to make along the way as it developed. Unit 3, Investigating Small Businesses, follows this through by asking you to apply your knowledge to a business that you are asked to study.

The fact you are studying Unit 2 means you are working towards the full GCSE in Business Studies, rather than one of the other options that are available. By the end of your course you should have a complete overview of business studies. You will be aware of how both small and large businesses operate, and you will be well placed to take the subject further, should you wish to do so. This might be at AS level, or by following a vocational business course.

You should by now have spent time studying Unit 1, Setting up a Business. Many of the topics that you will be meeting in Unit 2 have similar titles to those found in Unit 1. Do not think that you will be covering the same work, however. What Unit 2 does is:

- Extend your understanding of the topics by considering how they apply to larger businesses

- Look in more detail at the topics, so you have a firmer understanding of them and are able to use them in different circumstances.

When the specification was written by a team of writers at AQA, Unit 1 was intended to provide you, the student, with enough information to understand the basics of running a small business. After all, many young people study the subject because they feel they might want to run their own business at some stage in the future.

Most large businesses started life as small organisations, but have developed into much more powerful concerns. These companies tend to have many of the same problems as those experienced by a small business, but at a much bigger scale. The way that they go about dealing with these challenges is covered in Unit 2. It shows how the business could grow, and the changes that it would have to make along the way. It might need a different legal structure, for example, or its growth might cause problems amongst its stakeholders. As it grows, it is likely to change its targets: personal success or independence may no longer be enough; the business might want to become the biggest in its market, or even to expand overseas. Much will change as the business grows – the marketing mix will be different, larger businesses are financed differently and, with larger and more complex organisational structures, might need to be organised more formally. In Unit 2, you will also be developing your understanding of those business terms and ideas that apply more to larger companies.

Finally, in Unit 3, you will use all that you have learned to investigate a real business and present those investigations in a professional – businesslike – manner.

The examination papers

The GCSE course will be assessed by a combination of controlled assessments (see page 146) and exams.

You may already have taken the first exam, Unit 1. If you have, we hope you are satisfied with your result. You can, of course, retake the paper if you wish to try and improve upon your grade; this is something you will need to discuss with your teacher.

Some schools prefer their students to sit all three assessment components (the Unit 1 exam, the Unit 2 exam and the Controlled Assessment) in their final year of study, so you may not have taken any formal assessments yet.

The Unit 1 and Unit 2 exam papers have been purposely designed to have a similar feel, even though Unit 1 looks at small businesses and Unit 2 large businesses. Each paper will consist of about three separate questions, based on their own short case study. Each of the questions will have three or four parts or sub-questions. These get more challenging as you work through them, so be prepared for that. The number of marks for each sub-question tends to increase as you work down the list, indicating that more depth needs to be included in your answers to gain these marks.

Early questions are mainly descriptive, assessing your knowledge of business ideas and terms. The later questions assess your ability to apply that knowledge, or in other words to use it in different situations. These questions are also designed to get you to explore your own thoughts on the case study and consider alternative solutions to any problems that have been identified. These skills are called analysis and evaluation.

You will be asked to read the case study and then answer the questions that follow. The case study could contain clues to help you with your answers, but its main purpose is to set the scene for the questions. The nature of business studies means that there are often different interpretations and solutions to problems. The people who mark your scripts (completed exam papers) are aware of this and will reward you for answers that have been considered and are realistic. So be creative and try to find your own way through the questions. Just make sure you support everything you say with solid business ideas.

Both papers have up to 60 marks available. Individual sub-questions can be worth as few as 2, and as many as 10 marks. Use the number of marks available to help guide you on how much detail is needed in your answer. The amount of available space on the question paper is another important clue.

Make sure that you are familiar with the 'command words' in the questions. These are the instructions, such as state, give, describe, explain, advise and comment. These words are the biggest clues as to what skills (knowledge, understanding, application, analysis and evaluation) the examiner is looking for in your answers.

Finally, remember that, as with other GCSEs, your examiner will look at the standard of your written English and the presentation of your work. The answers to certain questions will be used to assess your writing skills, and marks will be awarded: check the front cover of the exam paper to see which questions will be used.

Acknowledgements

Every effort has been made to trace the copyright holders of quoted material. The publishers apologise if any sources remain unacknowledged and will be glad to make the necessary arrangements at the earliest opportunity. The authors and publishers would like to thank the following for permission to reproduce copyright photos:

Title page, Olga Zorina/iStockphoto.com; p.1 © cogal/iStockphoto.com; p.5 Rob Cousins/Alamy; p.6 © Arcaid/Corbis; p.11 Kumar Sriskandan/Alamy; p.13 MAURICIO LIMA/AFP/Getty Images; p.17 © Michał Kram/iStockphoto.com; p.19 © Bakaleev Aleksey/iStockphoto.com; p.22 Edward Moss/Alamy; p.23 © Photodisc/Getty Images; p.24 david pearson/Alamy; p.29 © Marcela Barsse/iStockphoto.com; p.30 © Gino Santa Maria/iStockphoto.com; p.32 ©Photodisc/Getty Images; p.33 © Sergey Lavrentev/iStockphoto.com; p.36 © Quavondo Nguyen/iStockphoto.com; p.39 Oleksiy Maksymenko/Alamy; p.40 Hugh Threlfall/Alamy; p.42 INTERFOTO Pressebildagentur/Alamy; p.44 David Cannon/Getty Images for Dubai Sports City; p.45 John Peters/Manchester United via Getty Images; p.50 Michael Ochs Archives/Getty Images; p.52 © Tony Tremblay/iStockphoto.com; p.54 © iStockphoto.com; p.57 © endrille/iStockphoto.com; p.58 © Ralf Siemieniec/iStockphoto.com; p.61 David Beauchamp/Rex Features; p.63 © mark yuill – Fotolia.com; p.64 Peter Lawson/Rex Features; p.67 Luca Ghidoni/Getty Images; p.74 PAUL ELLIS/AFP/Getty Images; p.75 © Rafal Zdeb/iStockphoto.com; p.81 Mario Tama/Getty Images; p.84 © Design Pics Inc./Alamy; p.89 © Pavel Losevsky/iStockphoto.com; p.91 fStop/Alamy; p.92 © Don Bayley/iStockphoto.com; p.98 Jim Wileman/Alamy; p.99 © www.fotoie.com/iStockphoto.com; p.102 Greg Balfour Evans/Alamy; p.105 David J. Green – work themes/Alamy; p.107 © Lisa F. Young/ iStockphoto.com; p.111 © Dean Mitchell/iStockphoto.com; p.115 © David H. Lewis/iStockphoto.com; p.119 © N_design/iStockphoto.com; p.121 © Bulent Ince/iStockphoto.com; p.123 Kevin Foy/Alamy; p.125 © Jorgen Udvang/iStockphoto.com; p.126 © ricardo azoury/iStockphoto.com; p.129 Jonathan Player/Rex Features; p.130 Barking Dog Art; p.131 AFP/Getty Images; p.135 Christopher Furlong/Getty Images; p.136 Leon Neal/AFP/Getty Images; p.141 © The British Standards Institution 2009; p.144 (left) © Brasil2/iStockphoto.com, (right) © Alexander Raths/iStockphoto.com.

BUSINESS ORGANISATION

Chapter 1
Introduction to business organisation

In this section

Introduction to business organisation
Expanding as a business
Choosing the right legal structure
Business aims and objectives
Business location

In Unit 1 we concentrated on how small businesses operate. We looked at the legal side of business, how funds could be raised and other aspects such as marketing and dealing with staff. As businesses grow, we notice a change in the ownership. With a small organisation, the owner – the entrepreneur – tends to both own and manage the business. But as a business gets bigger, the owners are less likely to play a part in running their company.

Many owners of small businesses see what they have created as their baby. Often faced with challenges, the entrepreneur works long hours to establish the business. There is pride in the birth of the enterprise and relief at its survival. There will come a point, however, when things start to change. If the business becomes a partnership or a private limited company, other people will become part owners and their views must be taken into account. We see a shift in control of the business from a sole proprietor, who takes total control, to a group of people. At this point some compromises have to be made if the business is to continue to be successful.

With growth, we see issues arising that were probably not a concern when the business was small. Employing staff would be an example of this. A small business might not employ anyone but the entrepreneur and his or her immediate family. As a business grows, others will need to be taken on, which brings with it concerns. Employment laws are strict and it is not as easy to 'let staff go' as some people think. Employees' wages are also a cost of the business that need to be paid each week or month, even if the money coming in is low.

Should a business grow?

Many businesses see benefits in becoming bigger. Growth might even be one of an organisation's objectives. But let's be clear, not all businesses want to grow bigger. Some face restrictions that limit just how big they can become. However, it is a frequent objective of many entrepreneurs to own a larger business. For some the reason might be purely financial: bigger businesses can bring larger profits. Others associate growth with success and want to expand because of the message this conveys to others. The cost of making each item, or providing a service, can also fall as a business grows.

The market for a product can increase through clever marketing and changes in consumers' attitudes and preferences. But a point may be reached when a business will have to look to overseas markets if the home market has become saturated. Selling abroad brings with it a range of challenges for a business to overcome.

Do we 'go public'?

If a growing private limited company wishes to raise capital from selling shares, it will eventually have to accept that it cannot rely on obtaining this finance from existing shareholders. It is at this point that it must decide whether to 'go public'. While the process of becoming a public limited company is relatively straightforward, particularly when businesses can pay experts to complete the process for them, becoming a public limited company is not something that a business should enter into lightly. Businesses like the idea of being able to sell shares to the general public, but becoming a public limited company is not without its downside.

What about aims and objectives?

The aims and objectives of a small business are unlikely to be something that the owner stops to think about on a daily basis. What the owner wants from the business is probably the thing that drives him or her on each day. But the objectives of the business are probably so deep rooted in the owner's mind that decisions are almost instinctively made to realise these objectives. As many small businesses have the objective of reaching a certain profit, each decision is based on the business moving closer to that goal.

Large businesses also have aims and objectives, which set out the reason for the business's very existence. These are often published so that everyone who has an interest in the business, often called its stakeholders, is aware of them. Unfortunately, things never remain constant in business and if a business is to survive, it might need to review its objectives to see whether a change needs to be made. A company might have the objective of obtaining a stated profit one year. However, if a new competitor enters the market, this objective might become unachievable. The business might decide that the objective of maintaining a certain market share would now be more appropriate. If a business is to survive, it will need to be flexible with its objectives to take into account changing circumstances.

We might also want to question how sincere some companies' objectives are. Many businesses like to give the impression that they are ethical concerns. If competitors have taken this stance, a business may have no real choice but to follow suit. As a result, many large businesses have objectives that include social and environmental targets. While this might appear praiseworthy, is this perhaps a form of marketing rather than proof of a social conscience?

Where should the business be located?

For the sake of convenience, entrepreneurs tend to set up their businesses close to where they live. If nothing else, it is a way of keeping costs down. It is likely that the most important consideration for a small business is where its customers are. As the business expands there will be other factors that need to be kept in mind. Availability of raw materials and the costs of transport are just two of these things. A cost saving of 10p per item might be insignificant to a small business dealing with 500 items a month. But to a large business that produces half a million of these items monthly, it is equivalent to saving £50,000 a month. So, larger companies are more sensitive to cost savings than small businesses.

Chapter 2
Expanding as a business

Cadbury plc

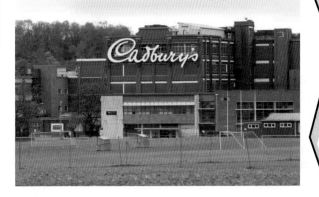

Cadbury, the well-known chocolate maker, has expanded as a business in several different ways. The company started back in 1824 when John Cadbury set up a tea and coffee shop in Bull Street in Birmingham. John introduced drinking chocolate and cocoa as drinks, which became popular with the people of Birmingham.

The business flourished over the next 50 years. Cadbury used its **retained profits** to pay to expand its business. In 1879, the business made a major decision and left the polluted centre of Birmingham and set up a factory, and later a workers' village, at Bournville. Cadbury always had the welfare of its employees at heart and wanted a healthier environment in which the workers could live and work. Bournville is four miles to the south of Birmingham and at the time was in the countryside and a pleasant place to live.

A major change to Cadbury came about in 1969 when the business merged with the soft drinks giant, Schweppes. The **merger** allowed both Cadbury and Schweppes to save money by sharing a management team. Other savings were made, for example sharing delivery lorries and a distribution network. The merger also allowed Cadbury to **diversify**. There followed a period when Cadbury Schweppes expanded by taking over other confectionery manufacturers. Some familiar names joined the Cadbury Schweppes stable of brands, including Dr Pepper, Bassett's, Trebor and Orangina.

Cadbury does not always manufacture the products that bear its name. Biscuits bearing the Cadbury brand, such as Cadbury Fingers, are produced under licence by another company. Ice cream based on Cadbury products, like 99 Flake, is made under licence by another business.

In May 2008, Cadbury Schweppes **demerged**. This means the business was broken down into two separate companies. Cadbury continued with confectionery products and the drinks side of the business became Dr Pepper Snapple Inc.

Take a look at the Cadbury website at
www.cadbury.com

Cadbury is a good example of an expanding business, as it has grown in several different ways.

Organic

Organic growth refers to the usually slow method of expanding by increasing output and sales. A business might decide to open a new shop or factory, take on more employees and produce more items for sale. Alternatively the organic growth might come about by using existing equipment and labour more productively, so the business does not actually grow physically bigger but more is produced. When this happens we say efficiency has been improved because more has been produced with the same **inputs**.

If a business has the objective of expanding rapidly, it's unlikely that organic growth would be the best strategy to achieve this. One of the other methods outlined below would be more suitable.

Mergers

Cadbury increased its size greatly when it merged with Schweppes in 1969. The two businesses manufactured different products, so were not in direct competition with each other. By merging, though, they were able to reduce their costs by sharing some of their resources. This avoided unnecessary duplication and helped make the profits of the Cadbury Schweppes company greater than the profits of the two separate businesses. When two businesses merge, it is not unusual for some employees and managers to be made **redundant**.

Takeovers

If a business wishes to expand quickly, it may decide to **take over** a competitor. This method of expansion not only allows a business to grow quickly; it has the extra benefit of removing a competitor from the market. Takeovers are sometimes called **acquisitions**, especially when the business being taken over is a private limited company. Taking over a public limited company (plc) involves buying enough shares in the business to take control of it. You will be looking more at **public limited companies**, or plcs, in the next chapter. If Cadbury were to buy half the shares in another confectionery business, it would be able to outvote the other shareholders. Cadbury could then vote for the new business to become part of the Cadbury group of businesses. Alternatively, Cadbury could persuade the board of directors that it would be in the shareholders' interests to be taken over. If the directors were convinced, they could recommend the takeover to the other shareholders.

Independent Newspapers needed this new building as the business grew

Franchising/licensing

If a business has a strong brand, as Cadbury has, it may allow, or license, other businesses to trade using its **brand name**. Cadbury does not actually make the cakes and ice cream that carry its name. Instead, other businesses make these products and in return for trading with the powerful Cadbury brand, they pay a **royalty**. While this is not technically expanding the amount that Cadbury produces, it provides a source of finance to the company.

Summary

- Businesses often want to expand as a way of increasing profits or achieving other objectives
- There are several ways in which a business can expand
- Many businesses expand organically, but if a faster growth rate is required, other methods might be used
- Growing as a business may bring in more profits, but there are risks associated with expansion

Did you know...

The world's biggest chocolate shop can be found at Cadbury World.

Core knowledge

Expanding their businesses is often seen as an attractive prospect to business owners. In simple terms the owners may think: if a business grows to twice its original size, it will make twice the profits. Unfortunately, the relationship between size and profits will probably not be as neat as the last sentence suggests. If conditions are wrong, a business might actually lose money if it grows, especially if it tries to grow too quickly. When this happens, we sometimes say the business has **overstretched** itself.

Overstretching can happen because a business owner has borrowed money to buy new equipment, machinery and premises and increased the business's costs as a result. The interest on the loan has to be paid off monthly, but it may take some time before new customers are found.

There are other reasons why owners want to expand their business, besides hoping to see an increase in profits. Business owners might want more control of the market than they currently have. Being the major business in an industry gives that company more scope to put up its prices, without losing customers to its competitors.

Expanding can also be a way of reducing the risks that a business faces. This is particularly the case when the expansion comes about by diversifying. Producing several products that are sold in different markets can spread risk: so, if one market fails, you have other products in other markets to fall back on.

Business owners might want to grow bigger because there is a good investment opportunity available to them. The owners might have discovered a gap in the market or a chance to increase sales. For instance, there has been an increase in the number of people keeping chickens and other poultry in their back gardens. This is because consumers are less willing to buy eggs from caged birds. A manufacturer of chicken coops or houses might decide to expand the business to be able to sell more while demand is high.

Many small businesses decide to grow organically. In order to be able to do this, a business needs finance to pay for new factories and other factors of production. There also have to be additional employees available. The market for the product or service must be large enough for consumers to be willing to buy the additional output of the business. If there is a limited demand for the product, or if there are many competitors, organic growth may be a problem. Of course, the demand for a product or service can be stimulated by price cuts, through effective advertising and by increasing the product range. If Cadbury were to simply make more products, there is no guarantee that they would be sold.

Many businesses use franchising as a way of expanding. Of course, for this to succeed, the business must have a good product that is respected by customers. The attraction of franchising is that the person who buys the franchise bears many of the risks. The franchisee puts money into the business, so the franchisor does not have to find the funding. If the business fails, it is the franchisee who suffers and not the franchisor. The franchisor is also paid a royalty payment for the privilege of letting another business use its brand.

Did you know...

Many of Cadbury's product brands have been around for a long time. Cadbury Dairy Milk, for example, was first produced in 1905, with Milk Tray starting in 1915 and Roses in 1938.

And more

When a business expands, there will be an effect on profit. Hopefully, the growth will result in more profits being made, but this might not be the case. Shareholders might have mixed views on their business expanding because of the risks involved.

The expansion will require funding, which will have an impact on shareholders. The funding could come from:

- **retained profits** – this will mean less money going to the shareholders. The shareholders might, however, be willing to sacrifice some money today to gain even more in the future;
- bank loan/mortgage – this source of finance would need to be serviced. This simply means interest will have to be paid on the amount borrowed, which will be an extra cost to the business;
- selling more shares – shareholders might be happy with this method to pay for the expansion, as they are not losing out directly. However, new shareholders mean the existing shareholders have less say in how the business is run. It will also mean that future profits have to be shared between a greater number of people.

How might shareholders react to business growth? Shareholders, like all people, will have different views on the matter. Some might be happy to take the risk for the reward of more dividends in the future; others might be more cautious and oppose growth, fearing it could lose rather than gain money. These shareholders could believe it would be difficult to attract new customers or new employees to produce the extra goods or services. They might worry about raising the money to fund the expansion, or about new shareholders joining the organisation.

Occasionally a large organisation might decide to split into two separate businesses. This is known as a demerger. The company might think it is becoming too large to function properly and it would be more profitable to operate as two independent concerns. Sometimes the split is forced by the government. This is usually because it is thought that the single large business has too much power in the market and customers are suffering through high prices and a lack of competition.

Sometimes a business will grow by producing more of the same product. This is known as horizontal growth. If Cadbury merged with another chocolate maker, this would be horizontal growth, or integration. Vertical growth refers to moving further up and down the production process. Cadbury buying a cocoa plantation in West Africa would be an example of vertical growth backwards. This is because cocoa is a raw material in chocolate making. If Cadbury decided to open up Cadbury shops to sell its products, this would be vertical growth forwards.

A benefit to a business of becoming larger is its costs per item can go down. We call this effect 'economies of scale'. But businesses can become so big that costs actually start to rise faster than the amount of extra goods being produced. This is the opposite of economies of scale and is called 'diseconomies of scale'. The whole topic of economies of scale will be dealt with later in this book.

Have a go!

Group activity

As a group, identify as many reasons as possible why a business might choose not to expand. Outline your reasons in a series of PowerPoint slides. Give your ideas as a presentation to the rest of the class.

Imagine you have an established business with a recognised brand name – you can choose a suitable product or service for this. Produce an A4-sized leaflet on the benefits of another business franchising your brand.

Discussion

Discuss how a business might recognise that it has grown so large it would be beneficial to demerge.

Quickfire questions

1   In which city did John Cadbury set up his tea and coffee shop?
2   What is the name of the Cadbury village?
3   Which company did Cadbury merge with in 1969?
4   What percentage of shares must a business buy in another company to have control of it?
5   What is a franchise royalty payment?
6   What is meant by diversifying?
7   What do we call it when a business has grown too quickly and is losing profits as a result?
8   Give two reasons why a business might not choose to grow bigger.
9   Explain what is meant by economies and diseconomies of scale.
10   Give an advantage to a business of expanding by vertical growth backwards.

Hit the spot

➤   Give two reasons why businesses want to expand.

➤➤   Explain two factors that limit how fast a business can grow.

➤➤➤   Discuss whether the bigger a business is, the more profits it will earn.

Cracking the code

Retained profit **That part of its profit used by a company to put back into the business, rather than be given to its shareholders.**

Merger **Two businesses joining together to save on their costs or reduce competition.**

Diversify **Produce a range of goods or services, which spreads the risk of the business failing.**

Demerger **Breaking up a business into two or more separate parts, each run independently.**

Organic growth **Growing by increasing turnover and sales.**

Inputs **The resources or factors of production that a business uses to produce its products.**

Redundant **When resources, such as members of the labour force, are no longer needed.**

Takeover **Taking control of another business by buying more than half of its shares.**

Acquisition **A business that has been taken over or bought by another company.**

Public limited company **A business that is allowed to sell its shares to anyone who wants to buy them.**

Brand name **A well-known company or product that consumers trust.**

Royalty **The fee paid to a business for using its brand name.**

Overstretched **When a business tries to grow too quickly, which can result in profits falling.**

Chapter 3
Choosing the right legal structure

Center Parcs

Center Parcs (UK) is a business that specialises in providing short-break holidays. The company owns four holiday villages around the UK, each set within a forest. The idea of forest holiday villages was developed by Dutch entrepreneur Piet Derkson, and the first Center Parcs village was opened in Holland in 1967. The business moved into the UK market in 1987, when the Sherwood Forest village was opened. Each village is based upon a large indoor swimming pool. There are many other leisure and sporting activities that the guests can enjoy, but these have an additional charge.

The chalet-style accommodation is self-catering, with guests able to cook for themselves, but there are several restaurants around the village for those who prefer to eat out. The main target market for Center Parcs holidays is families with higher-than-average incomes. The holiday company is also trying to attract business customers who use the facilities for conferences or team building.

It is very expensive for Center Parcs to build a holiday village. The company has to buy or lease the land and adapt it so that accommodation units can be built but without losing the attractiveness of the forest. There is also the cost of the domed swimming pool and other buildings and equipment. Center Parcs is in the process of building a new village at Warren Wood in Bedfordshire, scheduled to open in 2010. This new village will be smaller than the previous four villages, but it is estimated that it will cost about £160 million to complete the project.

Center Parcs' ownership has changed several times over recent years. The business was owned by Scottish and Newcastle (S&N) until 2001 when it was sold to allow S&N to concentrate on its core brewing business. In 2003 the owner of Center Parcs, Mid Ocean, sold the business once again to an organisation called Arbor. Center Parcs was then floated on the London Stock Exchange's Alternative Investment Market (**AIM**). This means Center Parcs was allowed to sell shares to the public, but without having to obey many of the regulations that the **Stock Exchange** imposes.

Center Parcs became a full public limited company (**plc**) in 2005. As a plc, Center Parcs did not have to limit its shareholders to those directly connected with the business – it was able to sell shares to the general public on the stock exchange. However, in 2006 the business was sold to the Blackstone Group of companies. The holiday business was brought back once again as a private limited company, with the support of its large parent company.

 Take a look at the Center Parcs website at **www.centerparcs.com**

Center Parcs has experienced many different types of legal ownership, particularly since 2001. The company had made the decision to expand organically by building another holiday village in Bedfordshire. The estimated £160 million it needed would have been very difficult to fund from existing shareholders. But as a private limited company it was not allowed to sell shares to anyone outside the organisation.

By becoming a public limited company (plc), Center Parcs would be permitted to sell its shares on the Stock Exchange to the general public. This would allow outside investors to put money into the business and more easily raise the large amounts of money needed.

Becoming a plc is neither a very expensive nor a complicated operation for a private limited business. It involves producing a number of documents and showing that the business is reliable. Many businesses, however, choose to use the services of a bank or an expert in these matters to guide them through the application. Once plc status has been achieved, the company is listed on the Stock Exchange and can begin to sell shares to anybody prepared to pay the going rate for them. We say that the business is now a quoted or listed company.

In the first part of this book, you will have read about what we mean by limited liability. You might remember that when the owners of small businesses want to expand, they will need to attract investors to put money into the business. These shareholders are technically owners of the business and are responsible for its debts. They probably have very little to do with the day-to-day running of the business, so feel that they should not be expected to have to sell their houses and other property to pay the company's debts. Limited liability grew from the need of investors to be protected from the creditors of the businesses in which they had bought shares.

If a private limited company wishes to raise additional capital it is not allowed to sell its shares to just anybody – only existing shareholders are allowed to put extra money into the business.

Did you know...

Sometimes people confuse a public limited business with the public sector. The two are quite different: the public sector is the businesses owned by the government, but plcs are owned by their shareholders.

Summary

- Private limited businesses that wish to raise large amounts of capital might choose to do this by becoming a public limited company (plc)
- There are disadvantages in becoming a plc and sometimes businesses return to being private limited companies

Core knowledge

Many private limited businesses are happy to remain as Ltd businesses. Becoming a public limited company may be a way to raise large amounts of capital, but being a plc can bring with it drawbacks for its owners.

It would be unreasonable to expect investors to part with their money unless they were confident that the business was stable and not likely to become bankrupt in the near future. To ensure that anyone thinking about buying shares is informed about the business, plc businesses must publish their **annual accounts** and send copies to anyone who requests them. To save the time and expense of this, most plcs publish their accounts on their websites.

This legal requirement to publish accounts does mean that competitors know exactly how well the business is doing. It provides them with information about the business's efficiency and whether new products, markets or advertising campaigns have been profitable. Many plc businesses would like to keep this type of information secret, but they are not permitted to do so.

As any person, or organisation, is allowed to buy shares in a plc, this means that competitors can buy the shares as well. Why should a competitor want to buy shares in another business? There is more than one reason for this. It may be simply a sort of insurance policy. If a business manages to attract other business's customers, then owning part of the successful company can provide some compensation to the one losing out. The loss in profits can be offset by the dividend payment from the thriving business.

Another reason could be the competitor is trying to take over the company in which it is buying shares. Once enough shares have been bought, the purchasing business can outvote other shareholders and take over the company. The company can then determine how the taken-over business operates, or even whether it closes down.

Buying and selling shares

The owners of some private limited companies are reluctant to go public for another reason. Some believe that public shareholders are more interested in earning quick profits rather than watching the business develop over a long period. This is a short-term view of buying shares – looking for a quick profit.

Shareholders are entitled to a share of their businesses' profits. This payment is called a **dividend**. Often businesses pay their dividends twice a year. Most of this money is paid when the accounts have been published and, quite often, some money is given to shareholders halfway through the year. This second dividend is often called an interim payment.

Not all profits are given to shareholders. After the profits have been calculated and all of the business's costs and tax liabilities have been paid, the company must decide what proportion of the profits to put back into the business. This money is needed to finance any expansion plans the company might have. The funds that are kept back are called retained profits. What is left is given out to the shareholders and is called distributed profits.

Did you know...

Many people incorrectly believe that when a business's share price fall, the business loses money. If the share price falls, the shareholder loses out, not the business.

Did you know...

Price rises and falls can be shown using index numbers, such as the FT 100SE, sometimes called the Footsie. This index measures the cost of buying shares in the top 100 businesses in the UK. The latest form of the Footsie began on 3 January 1984 when it was given the value 1000. When it reached 2000, shares, on average, had doubled in price.

And more

Businesses sell more than one type of share.

- *Preference shares*. The owners of preference shares have the right to be paid their dividends before other shareholders. They are usually paid a fixed amount each year for each share that they own. Because they are paid first there is less risk involved. As long as the business earns enough profit to pay its preference shareholders, they will be paid in full. Some preference shares are even cumulative. This means that if, for any reason, the business does not make enough profit to pay its preference shareholders, the shortfall will be made up the following year. This helps to reduce even further the risk of holding shares.

- *Ordinary shares*. Ordinary shares, as their name suggests, have no special rights or privileges. Ordinary shareholders have no guarantee that they will receive a dividend each year. Even if the business in which they hold shares earns a profit, it might decide to retain this profit, rather than distribute it to shareholders. Ordinary shareholders will receive what is left of the distributed profits after the preference shareholders have been paid.

The annual general meeting

- *Debentures*. Debentures are not really shares as the debenture holder does not receive a voting right. They are long-term loans to a business in exchange for a rate of interest, which will be the same each year. Some companies do not even pay this fixed rate of return. Sporting clubs occasionally fund some of the cost of their stadiums by selling debentures that guarantee a seat, rather than a rate of return. Examples include the All England Tennis and Croquet Club (Wimbledon), the Emirates Stadium (home of Arsenal Football Club), Lord's Cricket Ground, the Millennium Stadium and Wembley Stadium.

Most shareholders are happy to have nothing to do with the operations of the businesses in which they hold shares. As long as the business is paying a dividend which compares well with other similar companies, shareholders will often leave the business to get on with it.

Very few shareholders go to a company's annual general meeting (AGM). Many companies will interpret poor attendance at the AGM as shareholders being happy with the business so they have not bothered to go along. If a business is having problems, far more shareholders will attend, but still only a small percentage of all shareholders will be there.

Did you know...

The price a business's share trades for in the Stock Exchange changes many times during an average working day. If investors are confident that the business will make profits in the future, they will want to buy the shares, pushing up their price.

Have a go!

Group activity

Have a share-buying competition within your class. Working in small groups, decide how you would invest £100,000 in public limited company shares. Agree the rules that you will play to – for example, if there is a maximum number of companies, how often you can trade (sell or buy shares), and when the competition ends.

Each group should put their shares on a spreadsheet and use it to calculate the valuation. This should be repeated as share prices change. The winning team will be the group that has the highest share valuation at the end of the competition.

Discussion

Discuss ways by which Center Parcs might encourage business users to use its facilities.

Web-based activity

Produce a graph of how the value of the Footsie changes over the next two or three days. Try to explain any large changes by looking at news stories that could have influenced the price of shares.

Quickfire questions

1   What type of holidays do Center Parcs provide?
2   Who does Center Parcs target as its customers?
3   What is the estimated cost of building a new Center Parcs village?
4   Which company currently owns Center Parcs?
5   Where is the proposed site for the next Center Parcs village?
6   What is an AGM?
7   Give one difference between private and public limited companies.
8   Explain two differences between preference and ordinary shareholders.
9   Give two things that a company's shareholder might do if he/she thought the business was not making enough profit.
10 What does the Footsie measure?

Hit the spot

> What is meant by a public limited company (plc)?

> Explain an advantage of a business becoming a plc.

> Discuss whether going public is the best way for a business to raise large amounts of capital.

Cracking the code

AIM Alternative Investments Market. This is a group of businesses that sell shares to the public on the Stock Exchange. There are fewer regulations to obey with this type of listing.

Plc A public limited company. A business allowed to sell its shares to the general public.

Stock Exchange A place where shares can be bought and sold.

Annual accounts Financial details of a business, published each year.

Dividend The share of the profits that goes to each shareholder.

Chapter 4
Business aims and objectives

IN THE NEWS

In November 2008, Vodafone was voted the top company in a new set of awards that has been running for just five years. The award is called the Accountability Rating and measures how responsible companies are in the way they do business. In particular, it looks at how they have a positive impact on the societies and environments in which they operate.

Vodafone, the mobile network operator, is the largest telecommunications company in the world,

with an annual turnover of over £5 billion. As can be seen from the award, it is achieving one of its aims, which is linked to **corporate social responsibility (CSR)**. This is a measure of how well the business treats the communities and environments in which it works. The importance that Vodafone gives to CSR can be seen from the way it is included in its aims in both its mission statement and its vision statement. One way in which the business reduces its impact on the environment is by encouraging the recycling and re-use of mobile phones. In the UK there is one mobile phone for every man, woman and child in the population. Many of these are no longer used, so could be re-used in poorer countries or broken down and their parts recycled. Between 65% and 80% of a mobile can be recycled and re-used. When this includes some of the plastics, the total can be raised to 90%.

Vodafone is in partnership with Global Cool Foundation UK, a registered charity, Solar Aid, and The Million Superheroes Campaign. Each has a target linked to CSR. The Global Cool Foundation aims to reduce CO_2 emissions by 1 million tonnes; Solar Aid works to provide solar devices in sunny but poor African countries; and Superheroes wants to persuade 1 million people in the UK to sign up to become a Superhero and reduce their carbon emissions. The company sees CSR as central to its aims and produces a yearly CSR report to say how it has hit targets and what new targets it will set.

Go to **www.vodafone.com/start/ responsibility.html** and read about the areas in which Vodafone is trying to be responsible. Rate them in order of which you think is most important.

Changing aims

As a business grows, its aims and objectives are likely to change. You have already learned about how a business may start with aims such as survival, breaking even or making a modest profit. Once it has achieved these aims, it may then want to think about setting itself new aims, targets that may be harder to reach or take longer to achieve.

Why grow?

Some businesses never grow – because they serve a small market (like a local newsagent), for instance, or provide a specialist service. Others aim to grow to increase their share of the market, so that they can compete more effectively, perhaps take market share from rivals and also protect themselves from competitors.

As a business grows it may find that its home market is no longer big enough for it and so will look for ways to expand elsewhere. It can either expand through **diversification** – that is, moving into markets for other products or into other markets, physically separated from its current market. If it diversifies, it may do this in markets that are similar to the ones it is in (for example, National Express, the bus company, moving into operating as a train company) or it may move into completely new markets (for example, Whitbread, the brewers, moving into the fast-food market with Pizza Hut and the health market with David Lloyd Health Clubs).

Market dominance

Often a business which decides to compete in a particular market may be aiming to become the leading or **dominant business** in that market. This may give it many advantages over its competitors. It may become the preferred business of suppliers, or of retailers who see market size as a good indicator of success (or of ability to pay). It may become the leading brand and therefore the best known business in its particular market. It may be in a position to put pressure on suppliers to keep prices low, or to prevent other businesses from competing in the market. If, for example, every town has a major supermarket (such as Tesco), then it becomes increasingly difficult for other supermarkets to compete and almost impossible for smaller retail outlets to grow into the same market.

Overseas expansion

If a business moves into overseas markets, it will face new competition, language barriers, different laws and regulations, different transport and location problems and the need to employ local staff. Each of these areas will need to be addressed with new aims and objectives, and new policies to make sure that the business is competing effectively, efficiently and legally.

Ethics

Growing businesses, such as Vodafone, will also have to take into account ethical and environmental considerations. '**Ethics**' and being 'ethical' means 'doing the right thing'. In business terms it means not harming the places or communities where it works and not taking advantage of poorer countries or markets. Vodafone does this as part of its corporate social policy. The business must also consider the environment. This means aiming to do as little harm to the environment as possible. One part of this is to reduce its **carbon footprint**. The carbon footprint is the total amount of carbon dioxide (CO_2) and other greenhouse gases (gases that

harm the environment) that are produced over the lifetime of a product (or by an organisation). For a mobile phone this includes the raw materials, the energy used in manufacture, transport, storage, marketing and the eventual disposal of the phone.

It is in the interests of businesses to consider these as they are important to consumers and other stakeholders. A business that looks after the environment and has a low carbon footprint is one that is likely to be more attractive because it is being more responsible.

The disposal of an old phone contributes to its carbon footprint

Did you know...

Businesses can also grow by moving into different sectors of the market, which they have not targeted previously. For example, Wilkinson, the high street shop, decided to encourage students to shop there by targeting them through their universities. This was a part of the market that did not previously shop at the store, but which was encouraged to do so.

Summary

- As a business grows, its aims and objectives are likely to change
- Businesses can grow in different ways, e.g. into new markets or new locations
- Aims for a growing business could include increased market share or market domination
- Businesses will need new aims if they expand overseas
- Two key aims for modern businesses are to be ethical and environmentally responsible

Core knowledge

All businesses have aims and objectives. Often these are written down in the 'mission statement' or 'vision' of the business. The longer-term objectives are usually broken down into smaller, shorter-term targets, or aims. As a business grows, it will have to consider wider aims than those that it had when it was smaller. Aims and objectives will alter not only as the business grows but also according to how the business has decided to grow. The increased size of a growing business will immediately give it more responsibilities and these will need to be reflected in its aims. Examples include:

- if it begins to operate in overseas markets, it will need to take account of local laws and regulations, customs and holidays, and matters of transport and communication;
- if it has a larger or more diverse workforce, it will need to take into account differences in culture, working conditions and wage rates, and the need to treat all of its employees equally, no matter where they are working;
- if it gains new groups of stakeholders, it will need to take into account their interests. In particular, it will gain new customers whose loyalty it will need to work on, new communities in which it works and possibly new investors concerned with profits and returns.

One of the most important considerations for many businesses, but especially growing ones, has become environmental and ethical considerations. Customers, suppliers, shareholders, governments and other stakeholders want to see that a business is being responsible in many different ways. Businesses are expected to treat all of their workers equally, no matter where in the world they work. They are also expected to be as good to the environment as possible, for instance, looking for green sources of energy or better ways to dispose of waste. Many also provide for the communities where they work by paying for services such as education or health care.

And more

The main aim of almost all businesses is to make a profit. Some social enterprises (like charities or co-operatives) may aim to maximise the good that they do, but even with these types of organisation it is important to make sure that costs are lower than revenues. Other businesses claim many aims and objectives. Some commentators would say that, looking at the early – and basic – aims of a small business, and comparing these with the aims and objectives of a growing business, there are not any that are not directly linked to profit.

In its early days a business may look to survive or break even – it can do this only if it makes enough money to buy stock, market its products and pay the wages of its staff (including the owner). In the longer run, aims such as corporate social and environmental responsibility, increased market share and international expansion may all be considered as ways to make more profit. If a business is a significant player in a market, it can compete more effectively, take a greater market share, introduce new product lines and target new customers – all of which could be profitable. If its customers are happy, then they will return to buy more products and recommend the business to friends, so good customer service becomes a key part of profitability. If the business is good to the communities and people where it works, it is likely to be more efficient and therefore more profitable. It may therefore be true to say that if a business hits its aims of efficiency, environmental responsibility and growth, it is also likely to increase profit.

Have a go!

Group activity

Visit **www.direct.gov.uk/actonCO₂** where you can calculate your carbon footprint. Compare this with other members of your group. Find out how you could reduce your footprint and calculate how much carbon you could save for your whole group.

Discussion

Find out what the 'mission statement' or 'vision statement' is for your school or college. Discuss whether or not you agree with it and how you would alter it. If your school or college does not have a statement, then agree the details of one for it.

Web-based activity

Visit a selection of 5–10 websites of leading companies and list their aims and objectives. Group them into similar types of aims (e.g. efficiency, profitability, returns to investors, corporate responsibility, innovation). See which are the most common aims and say why you think this is so.

Quickfire questions

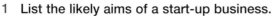

1   List the likely aims of a start-up business.
2   List the likely aims of a growing business.
3   What is meant by 'diversification'?
4   What is market dominance?
5   Give two possible new responsibilities of a growing business.
6   List two possible advantages of moving into overseas markets.
7   List two possible disadvantages of moving into overseas markets.
8   Explain what is meant by 'ethics'.
9   Why is an ethical approach important to some businesses?
10 What is a carbon footprint?

Hit the spot

> Give two reasons why a business may decide that it does not want to grow.

>> Explain what is meant by a market leader or dominant business in a market. Explain why a business would want to be in this position.

>>> Is it true to say that all aims and objectives are linked to profits? Explain how you have come to your conclusion.

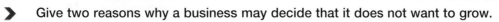

Cracking the code

Carbon footprint The amount of greenhouse gases or CO_2 released during the life of a product or related to a particular activity.

Corporate social responsibility (CSR) A measure of how well the business treats the communities and environments in which it works.

Diversification When a business moves into markets for other products or into other markets.

Dominant business or market leader The leading business in a particular market because it has the largest share of the market.

Ethics The idea of 'doing the right thing' and not harming the places or communities where a business is located.

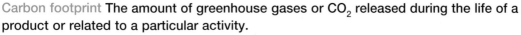

Chapter 5
Business location

Aston Science Park is a specialist location for science- and technology-based industries. It was founded by Birmingham City Council, Lloyds Bank and Aston University in 1982 and is recognised worldwide as a leading science park. It is home to a number of businesses that can benefit from the research facilities of Birmingham's Aston University, which shares the site with them. The businesses can work in partnership with the University, making use of its expertise and research facilities. In 2008, this led to science park business Arden Photonics and Aston University winning a major award for a development that will help to make fibre optic cables more efficient.

The University runs what it calls a 'Knowledge Transfer Initiative', in which it works with businesses in order to share and transfer knowledge between the business and research sectors. Aston represents the research part of this link, while the Science Park attracts the right sort of 'cutting edge' businesses to take advantage of such research. Representatives of both the University and the businesses have praised the location and the partnership. Dr Kate Sugden, Senior Lecturer of the Photonics Research Group at Aston University, commented: 'Aston University has a well deserved reputation for its highly successful knowledge transfer activities with regional companies and we're pleased that this award will raise our profile still further.'

Arden Photonics itself, Aston University and other businesses located on Aston Science Park were pleased with the award, which they said would raise the profile of the Park still further and enhance its reputation. Everyone was looking forward to working together in the future at what is seen as a prestigious and successful location.

 Visit **www.astonsciencepark. co.uk/about-us.html** to see the main types of companies that are located at the science park. Using this information, define what you think is the purpose of a science park.

Type of business

Location is an important factor for many businesses, but just how important depends on the type of business and the goods or services that it produces. A business needs to look at two major elements.

The first are the **factors of production** that it needs to produce its good or service. A manufacturer may need to be close to raw material supplies, or to a reliable power source. A wholesaler may need to be close to a good distribution network such as a railway or motorway system. Power, transport and other vital services are called '**infrastructure**'.

The second is its market. A retailer may need to be close to its market, but will also need to be close to transport so that goods can be delivered. For some businesses, therefore, geographical location is important – for example, raw material extraction can only take place where the raw materials are located. For other businesses, geographical location may be of little or no importance. An internet selling operation needs an internet connection and to send products out from warehouses or distribution centres, but may be located almost anywhere in the world. Businesses selling a service need to be close to customers if this is a personal service (like haircutting) but may be located anywhere if it is information or advice related or similar. For example, the actual location of an online bank, insurance company or tax adviser is of no importance to the quality or availability of the service.

International businesses will need transport links

Key questions

A business seeking a location must therefore be able to answer the following questions:

- What space do I need?
- What facilities (such as IT and storage) do I need?
- What transport links do I need?
- What labour, including specialists or specialisms, do I need?
- How close to my customers do I need to be?
- How much am I willing to pay?

International expansion

Businesses might also grow by expanding internationally or even globally. Sometimes this means that they will have to establish a physical presence in a different country. Overseas locations can bring their own advantages and disadvantages. The main decision regarding location will be whether to **export** from the current location or to set up a new base in the overseas country or countries in which the business is operating. Each has possible benefits and drawbacks, so the choice is a crucial one.

If the business is a manufacturing company, it may make sense to continue to produce where there are established raw material supplies, existing machinery and trained labour. However, if costs are lower in the new country, it could make sense to establish the business there. This also cuts out the costs of transporting the products. The disadvantage of such a move could be that the new country has different laws or regulations, or charges more in taxation. There could also be language difficulties. Businesses also have to decide whether it is best to put their own people into the new country or employ locals. Their own people will be trained and experienced but may not speak the language or know the customs of the country. New people will need to be trained and this could prove costly.

Businesses can also decide on a 'middle way' which is to use **agents** in the new country.

These have the advantage of local knowledge and language skills and do not need a lot of training from the business. The disadvantage is that they are not actually employees of the business, so may not always be working in its best interests.

Did you know...

Not only does the UK government provide assistance for businesses to locate in the UK, but the European Union provides assistance for businesses to locate in various poorer parts of Europe.

Summary

- Location may be an important factor for a business
- How important will depend on the type of business
- All businesses will locate with the intention of keeping costs down
- Generally, businesses need to be close to raw materials or close to their markets
- Businesses have to ask key questions about cost and availability of resources before choosing a location
- International expansion brings a whole new set of location decisions

Core knowledge

When a business first starts, a correct choice of location is often central to its success. A small business may need to be convenient to its customers. Later, the growing business will look at location in terms of keeping costs as low as possible while increasing revenues. Costs can be kept low by locating either near the market or near the raw materials, depending on the product being sold. Costs can also be kept down by being near infrastructure and by taking advantage of government grants. Revenue can be increased by being able to sell at convenient locations. Some locations will attract customers because there are other businesses of the same type at that location. For example, a computer or electrical

An overseas call centre

goods shop will attract more custom if it is on a retail estate with similar shops. Customers will be attracted to a group of shops so that they have a choice. Costs may be reduced by locating certain operations where they are cheapest. This could mean setting up a central storage or distribution depot, for example, or locating some services overseas. Many call centres are now located in India, as this is cheaper than paying similarly qualified staff in the UK.

There are also historical factors that affect the location of a business. If an area has a tradition of, for example, shoe manufacture (Leicester) or fine textiles for suits (Huddersfield), then other businesses, producing similar products, will be drawn to the same area. Even though the original reasons for such a location may have vanished, there will be other factors – such as the availability of trained labour – that still attract businesses.

Businesses may also receive help from national or local government in the form of grants or lower rents or rates to encourage them to certain areas. These may be, for example, areas of high unemployment or where there has been a decline in traditional industries.

Did you know...

For some businesses, a single location factor is of great importance. Textile mills, for example, had to be located near fast-flowing rivers both to provide power and to clean textiles.

And more

Different businesses may be pulled or pushed towards a particular type of geographical location. For example, a manufacturing business may be pulled in a different direction to a retail business. Some businesses are drawn more towards locations near their markets. These are often **bulk decreasing industries**. If a product loses weight, size or bulk during the manufacturing process, then it makes sense to do most of the work – such as manufacturing, refining and processing – as near to the raw material source as possible. The business can then reduce costs by being able to transport the product when it is less bulky. So the best place for refining oil is on the coast, where the oil is landed, or even on an oil rig. (This is also a dangerous process so should take place away from centres of population.) Some businesses, meanwhile, operate in what are called **bulk increasing industries**. It is much easier and cheaper to transport wood to as near to the customer as possible before manufacturing furniture, which may be delicate and is certainly more bulky. The journey to the retailer is thus relatively short.

Businesses can take advantage of international locations to help keep costs down. For example, a business that has production and sales bases in a number of countries may be able to take advantage of local labour rates, or health and safety regulations. It may also be able to choose to pay its taxes in the country that has the lowest levels of taxation. Sometimes this is seen as unfair and, in recent years, there have been many controversies. These often involve the use of cheap (even child) labour and unsafe working conditions where businesses have been accused of taking advantage of poorer or less developed countries.

Did you know...

Some businesses need to be located where they will do least harm if something goes wrong. Nuclear power plants, for example, are located away from major centres of population.

Have a go!

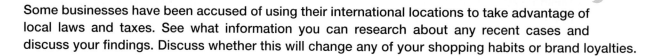

Group activity

Find out the difference between a greenfield site and a brownfield site. What are the advantages and disadvantages for businesses and local communities of locating on either?

Discussion

Some businesses have been accused of using their international locations to take advantage of local laws and taxes. See what information you can research about any recent cases and discuss your findings. Discuss whether this will change any of your shopping habits or brand loyalties.

Web-based activity

Use the internet to investigate a local retail park or shopping centre and list all of the shops there. See how many of them are selling similar goods. Explain why you think this is so.

Quickfire questions

1   Name the factors of production.
2   What is meant by 'infrastructure'?
3   Name two services that have to be close to the customer.
4   Name two services that can be geographically distant from the customer.
5   Give one way in which a growing business can use location to keep costs low.
6   Give one way in which a growing business can keep costs low.
7   Give one way in which a growing business can increase revenue.
8   Give two possible problems with overseas locations.
9   Give one advantage and one disadvantage of using an agent.
10 What is the difference between bulk increasing and bulk decreasing industries?

Hit the spot

➤   Give two reasons why a business might need to locate near to its market.

➤➤   Explain why a business might decide to keep production in the UK and export goods rather than set up a plant overseas.

➤➤➤ An expanding business must ask key questions about its location. Which of these questions is the most important? Explain why you think so.

Cracking the code

Agents Anyone in business acting on behalf of another person, business or organisation.

Bulk decreasing industries Where the manufacturing or processing process makes goods smaller, or easier to transport.

Bulk increasing industries Where the manufacturing or processing process makes goods bigger, or harder to transport.

Export When goods or services are sent out of one country to another (the receiving country imports them).

Factors of production The inputs needed by a business in order to produce – land, labour and capital.

Infrastructure The availability of services that help businesses: a good infrastructure provides sources of power, transport and communications.

SECTION 2

ADVANCED MARKETING

Chapter 6
Introduction to advanced marketing

In this section

Introduction to advanced marketing
The marketing mix: product
The marketing mix: price
The marketing mix: promotion
The marketing mix: place

Marketing mix

This section uses marketing ideas – in particular the marketing mix of product, price, promotion and place – and looks at how each (and combinations of each) might change as a business grows. The marketing mix is the balance of its four elements as used by a business. These are the product itself (product could be either a good or a service), place (where the good or

Each element of 'the mix' is important in its own right – but more so when combined with the others, like mixing paint on a palette

service is available, or methods by which a business can get it to the customer), price, which must be competitive (i.e. within the customer's range for such a product) and promotion – telling people about the product.

Balance

It is the balance of the marketing mix that is more important than any of the individual elements. Without products to sell, there is no point in setting a price. A competitive price – i.e. one where consumers will consider the product is worth buying – is necessary to attract customers. Promotion is necessary to tell customers of the existence of products and to persuade them to buy. Place includes both where the products are sold (everywhere from online to market stalls) and how the products are distributed to consumers. Distribution and location are important to create somewhere where buyers and sellers can come together to complete the sale. This means that there must be a place where customers can come to buy, or the business must be prepared to distribute products to an appropriate place.

A marketing mix is not fixed for any particular period of time. It has to be fluid, something that has to keep changing as circumstances change. Businesses are constantly adapting their marketing mix to try to improve their performance. Sometimes this is in response to competitor actions, sometimes in response to changes in the market. Businesses that grow will do so as a result of changing their marketing mix and gaining the benefits from these changes. A new product line, a price reduction, a successful promotion, a new distribution strategy (such as opening up internet sales) can all lead to growth. Businesses can also grow by moving into new markets, sometimes linked to the ones in which they currently operate, sometimes in completely new directions.

The role of market research

Businesses will, of course, use market research to find out about the possible changes in their market (or to find out how best they can bring about change in their market). They will gather information on who currently buys the product, who might be persuaded to buy it in the future, what competitors are doing, how the market is changing and how they might take advantage of those changes. They can look at how markets are divided (or 'segmented') and how they can turn this to their advantage. No sensible business would embark on a growth strategy without good market research information to back them up.

Growth

It is worth, here, taking a brief look at what is meant by growth in relation to markets and how it might happen. As business size can be measured in several different ways, so businesses can grow in several different ways. Size may be measured through number of employees, value of assets, stock market valuation, size of sales revenue or share of market. You need to investigate the type of business and type of market before you can say whether a business is small, medium or large – and whether or not it has grown. For example, an engineering firm is likely to have a lot of assets by way of machinery and factories, but may employ few people. (The use of robots and automated systems in

manufacturing may mean that large engineering companies inevitably have high-value assets but few employees.) A service-based industry (such as a postal delivery or courier service), meanwhile, may have many employees but little in the way of tangible assets. You should also be sure, if using market share as a guide to growth, that it is the business that has grown rather than the market that has shrunk. A 20% share of £1 million market is £200,000. If the market shrinks to £500,000 but market share rises to 25%, the share is now worth £125,000. Has the business grown or not? Looking just at market share, the business would appear to have grown – comparing it with changes in the market, you can see that this is not the case.

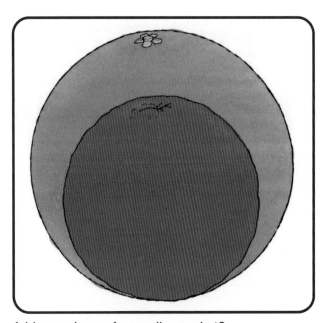

A bigger share of a smaller market?

Where does growth take place?

Internal growth is a direct result of changes to the marketing mix – for example, an increase in sales, the use of new technology in its production processes that allow the business to expand its product range, or by using promotion to tap into bigger market shares. External growth is when a business grows by joining up with other businesses. Sometimes this is when two businesses merge. Sometimes it is when one business takes over another.

SMEs

SMEs are a group of businesses that the government particularly targets for help as they are seen as the backbone of an enterprise economy and the most likely to grow in the future. SME stands for small and medium-sized enterprises. Many are very small so-called micro businesses, with fewer than ten employees, but the definition includes businesses employing up to 249 people.

A small, local business

Staying small

Of course, not every business wants to grow. A business that has just started may be more concerned with ensuring its survival, and may be happy to provide a local service or supply specialist products to small markets. In some cases, the type of business is such that there is little opportunity to expand – local services like window cleaning or gardening are likely to stay local rather than seek to establish national chains.

Chapter 7
The marketing mix: product

Mobile phones – and the ringtones that owners download to go with them – may now be considered a **mature market** in the UK. The mobile phone market in the UK would find it difficult to expand its basic service through increased ownership of mobile phones. As long ago as 2003, it was reported (by telephone regulator Oftel) that over 90% of 15–34 year olds in the UK owned at least one mobile phone and that ownership even in the youngest category – the 7–10 age group – was at 25% and rising rapidly.

Monstermob is a growing business that has done well out of this increase. It is a content provider based in Lancashire, with one of its biggest lines being mobile phone ringtone downloads. Every phone has, of course, at least one ringtone, but most have several. Some have even entered the music charts they have been so popular. (Crazy Frog, for example, earned over $28 million for the firm that released it and even had its own album!) Some are seasonal (especially Christmas jingles), while others, like current pop songs, are temporary. In other parts of the world, expansion through increased ownership is still feasible (although all but the poorest countries are rapidly catching up), so Monstermob needs to find a way of extending the product life cycle for the ringtones it produces.

One way to do this would be to provide more content, but, of course, this is expensive. Another is to find different markets in which to sell existing content. Monstermob decided that the best way to extend the life of its product was to sell ringtones into those markets where phone ownership is on the increase, but ringtones and other content have not yet become popular. To do so, it bought up providers in Malaysia, China and the Philippines, along with Russian content provider Mobicon. The biggest of these markets are China and Russia. Russia has widespread ownership of mobile phones, but people use them for calls and texts rather than entertainment, while the Chinese market is estimated to be some six years behind the European one. Monstermob's acquisitions have allowed it to extend the life cycle by introducing the product to completely new markets.

 Looking at the figures for 2007/8 at **www.csu.nisra.gov.uk/Mobile_ phone_ownership_by_sex_and_ age_Trend.htm**, which section of the market would you suggest a mobile phone company could target? Suggest the sort of campaign that might attract this sector or age group.

Growth

The **product** is often said to be the most important part of the **marketing mix**. Without the product, there is no need for promotion, no price to set and no location or distribution needed. Businesses may grow by increasing the sales of a product, or by expanding into new products. Monstermob has, in the past, grown through first providing ringtones, then a range of ringtones, and then by targeting markets where demand is set to grow (and also where competitors are not yet strong).

Changes in demand

Demand for a product is not static but will be changing all the time. Changes are caused by changes in taste or fashion, new products coming on to the market, changes in price and changes in income and spending patterns. As a business gains market share or becomes more profitable, it may feel that it can bring new products into its range. Monstermob is still developing products such as different novelty ringtones and better quality ones. For example, early ringtones were 'two tone', later ones (as mobile phone technology has improved) now have full music quality. Sometimes a business may feel that it needs to broaden the range available, sometimes to balance what may seem a one-sided product mix. Any business which has a narrow product range is vulnerable to changes in demand, so needs to either develop new products or target new markets.

How being bigger helps

A larger business is able to support a wider product portfolio so is better able to compete. It can support the introduction of new lines with the profits from existing ones. It may also be able to gain **economies of scale** – discounts from buying, selling or transporting in larger amounts. Such gains (or at least part of them) may then be passed on to customers in the form of lower prices.

Product life cycle

The demand for a product – the number of people who wish to buy it and think the price is reasonable – will alter over time. Often this is due to the natural '**product life cycle**'. A product, once launched, passes through various stages – growth, maturity, market saturation and finally decline (see the figure below). Different product life cycles are possible and businesses have to try to take advantage of them as best they can. They can be exceedingly long or very short. A long life cycle might mean a product that grows slowly but steadily, but provides a good income over a number of years. Some products will still be selling hundreds of years after their launch – tobacco has been around since the 16th century but only recently have sales started to decline. If businesses predict a short life cycle, they need to reap as much from it in a short time period as possible. A novelty seasonal item (such as a Christmas Number 1 chart hit) will find sales vanishing on December 26th.

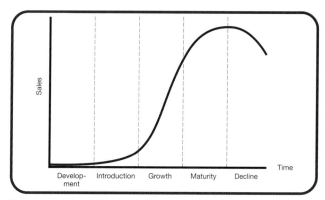

Product life cycle

Changing marketing mixes

At each stage of the life cycle, the business can use different marketing mixes to support sales. At the launch or growth stage, promotional prices may be used and there may be heavy spending on advertising. Once the product reaches maturity and competitors enter the market, there may be additions to the product or variations on it. Prices may also have to fall in response to competition.

Extending the life cycle

A product can benefit from additions, alterations or modifications that extend the life cycle. Methods that a business might use to extend the product life cycle include:

● cosmetic changes – changing packaging or the look of a product;

● real changes – introducing new versions of the product;

● technological change – making more advanced versions of the product, with more technological features;

● finding new uses for a product;

● extra promotional activities;

● adding to the product range.

Each method has to be carefully considered by the business, as any product development could have an impact on other lines. All the time, the business needs to make sure that it is supporting its various products in a balanced way. Sometimes a business just has to realise that the life cycle is at an end and let the product die. Once the iPod was launched, for example, this spelled the end for personal CD players.

Summary

● Product is just one part of the marketing mix, but an important part
● Growing businesses may need a bigger product range or a greater variety of products
● Products follow a product life cycle
● At each stage of the life cycle, other parts of the marketing mix may be changed to support the product
● Product life cycles follow the same stages, but can range from very long to very short
● There are various ways to extend product life cycles

Core knowledge

As the business grows it may feel that it should not rely on a single product but look at variations of the product, or at other product lines. The three main routes for expansion using products are expanded product range, product differentiation and diversification. Each will lead to a different product portfolio for the business. This is a reminder of what each of those terms means:

- *Product range*: this refers to the different lines that a business sells, such as a car manufacturer selling a range of cars. Look at any make of car and you will know that there is a range of models. At one end will be the small family saloon, at the other a luxury version. In between you will find hatchbacks, two- or four-door models and, of course, a huge range of colours.
- *Product mix*: this refers to the variety of products for sale. For example, Rolls-Royce Motors has a fairly narrow mix, concentrating on the luxury car market. Ford, meanwhile, has a wide mix, including cars at all levels, vans and commercial vehicles.
- *Diversification*: this is the process of expanding into product areas where the business did not previously have a presence. The Virgin group of companies shows how the business has diversified from its original product base (a record shop) into travel, leisure, banking, communications and other areas.

Monstermob has a single range of products and a very narrow mix. However, this is not a problem if it can enter growing markets where demand for ringtones is only just starting to grow.

And more

Products – goods or services – are provided to target all types of market. In each case, there are certain aspects of the product that are particularly important. Growing businesses need to concentrate on these aspects in relation to the markets that are their targets. One important aspect may be a strong brand. In some cases having a branded product may be important to a market – genuine car parts may be better than substitutes that may or may not do the job. In other cases a brand makes little difference. Does the brand of salt bought matter, for example?

Products provide tangible and intangible benefits at a number of levels. Tangible benefits are the 'real' benefits to owning or using a product. The tangible benefit from listening to an iPod is the enjoyment of the music. Intangible benefits are those that come with the product but are not part of its function. The intangible benefit of owning an iPod is the impression that you are a person with style. Benefits come at three levels. If you buy a laptop, for example, the core reason may be to do school or college work, so the core product is the one that has word-processing and spreadsheet programs. Maybe you also want it for games, so this

What is the *real* reason for buying a particular laptop?

would form part of the core. The secondary reason for buying that particular product will be a combination of design appeal, packaging, brand and other product features such as reputation and quality – the 'actual product' or 'tangible benefits'. At yet another level, the third or 'tertiary' reason might be linked to the product's availability and to guarantees of quality and customer support – this is called the 'augmented product' and is linked to the intangible benefits. Sometimes the augmented product is more important (the guarantees and service agreements on cars, for example), sometimes the core product (basic foodstuffs), sometimes secondary reasons like design (designer clothes are meant to make you look good, not necessarily keep you warm or comfortable, the core benefit of clothing).

Did you know...

A strong product identity is often linked to a strong brand name or image. If a business has a strong brand, it can transfer this to other products. A good example is the Virgin brand, which has been spread across many different businesses from travel and leisure to mobile phones and banking, or top sports brands like Nike, that have moved into branded bathroom products.

Have a go!

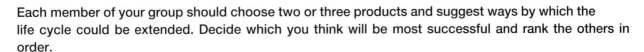

Group activity

Each member of your group should choose two or three products and suggest ways by which the life cycle could be extended. Decide which you think will be most successful and rank the others in order.

Discussion

Many people say that it is a waste to have so many different product types and ranges. For example, what is the point of having different coloured cars, or different fashions for clothes? It would be a lot more efficient to have things all the same. Discuss whether or not you agree with this point of view.

Web-based activity

Read the article at **www.guardian.co.uk/media/2006/jul/11/newmedia.citynews**. How do you think that this news will affect Monstermob in the long term? What strategy would you suggest the company adopts in order to recover?

Quickfire questions

1   What is meant by 'product'?
2   What is a 'product life cycle'?
3   Give three factors that cause changes in the demand for products.
4   What is 'diversification'?
5   What is meant by 'product portfolio'?
6   What are the stages of the product life cycle?
7   What is a narrow product range? What problems might this cause for the business?
8   What is the difference between a tangible and intangible benefit from a product?
9   Suggest two reasons why a strong brand may be important for a product.
10 Suggest three ways to extend a product life cycle.

Hit the spot

> Give two reasons why a business might change its marketing mix.

> Explain why a business might need to broaden and balance its product range.

> Which part of the life cycle do you think is most important to a growing business? Explain why you think so.

Cracking the code

Diversification Expanding into product areas or markets where the business did not previously have a presence.

Economies of scale Discounts from buying, selling or transporting in larger amounts.

Marketing mix The balance of product, price, promotion and place.

Mature market The point when most people who are likely to buy the product have bought it.

Product The good or service offered for sale by the business.

Product life cycle The various stages of sales through which a product passes, from launch to eventual decline.

Product mix The variety of products for sale.

Product range The different lines that a business sells.

IN THE NEWS

The Apple iPhone 3G, with built-in GPS* and Wi-Fi, itself a development from an earlier version, hit the market in 2008. By October of the same year, Blackberry had announced the launch of its latest 'smart' phone, the Blackberry Storm, also with 3G, built-in GPS and mobile broadband capability. As well as competing in the mobile phone and PDA** market, phones such as these could spell the death of separate satellite navigation devices (satnavs).

Satnavs are a good example of the type of pricing that can be used for new products. In November 2005, the most popular types were priced at around £350 – a price that 'skimmed' the market – attracting those who wanted to be first with the new technology. Even though there were several competing systems, this was a technological novelty so prices were not driven down.

Retailers maintained the price for as long as they could, as demand grew up to Christmas – and then, the **skimming** phase over, dropped it dramatically so that, by January 2006, you could pick up a Navman (a popular brand) for less than £200. Competition in the market such as that from the iPhone and the Storm is likely to drive prices down even further. Separate sales may also fall as car manufacturers decide that the satnav is the latest device that should be 'built in' to new cars. At the moment, the popularity of the portable ones is demonstrated by the fact that these are now the item most often stolen from a vehicle, but built-in ones will be much more secure.

Satnav manufacturers have managed to use a number of pricing strategies to keep sales of their product going, but may, in the end, have to accept that there is no longer a market for a portable satnav device.

 * Global Positioning System
** Personal Digital Assistant, also known as a palm-top device

 Go to
www.vodafone.co.uk/Storm and
www.apple.com/uk/iphone to find
out about the Blackberry Storm and the
iPhone 3G. What sort of pricing strategies

What is it worth?

How much would you pay for a satellite navigation system for a car? If you were buying one as a gift for an older brother or sister, or a parent, what would you be willing to pay? In other words, how much do you think a satnav is worth? If your answer is £200 to £250, then you would probably have bought one in 2006. If it is £40 to £50, then you might have considered buying one for Christmas 2008. This shows the range of prices that you will be looking at and hoping that a retailer agrees with your estimate.

When these devices first came on the market a few years ago, they were priced at a high level. If you were buying for Christmas 2005, for example, you could not expect to buy one for less than £350. This was a price intended to 'skim' or 'cream' the market. As a new, high-technology product, satnavs could be priced at a high price in order to make the most of the market. Even with a number of competing manufacturers, the price stayed high, especially in the run-up to Christmas, when the highest volume sales were made. With new technology products, there is often a group of consumers which sees them as a 'must have'. They are therefore willing to pay a high price. In January 2006, the price dropped to a more realistic £200 and has continued to fall.

By the start of 2009 models were available priced at around £50 and the satnav was no longer considered a luxury item. Many new car models now have them built in and they are likely to become a standard feature, like central locking, electric windows and airbags – all luxuries in their day. Also, GPS devices that operate in the same way are now being installed in mobile phones and PDAs.

Pricing strategies for growth

Businesses use a number of strategies to increase **market share** or to gain a foothold in new markets. These include:

- **loss leaders** – a business deliberately prices a product at a loss (a price that does not cover cost). This will attract customers to the business. Other strategies can then be used to try to develop customer loyalty to keep their custom;

- **skimming** – the product is sold at an initial high price to those customers ready to pay for it. These products are usually luxury items and often 'cutting-edge' technology. Examples include flat-screen TVs, DVD players, Blu-Ray players and satnavs. Once the initial surge in demand has gone, prices are dropped. In some cases, the products barely survive beyond the introductory phase as newer technology is brought out;

Satnav units had high prices at first

- **premium pricing** – this is when prices are set at a high level to try to emphasise the quality of the product – designer clothes, for example;

- **penetration price** – price is set below competitor prices so that a business can gain a share in a market. In some industries, customers are reluctant to change to competitors. (In the UK, people are very unlikely to change banks, for example.) Often penetration prices are short term and last only as long as the business needs to gain a place in the target market.

How being bigger helps

A larger business is able to make short-term losses on, for example, loss leaders or new products that it is introducing. It can also afford to charge promotional prices on certain lines, paid for by the profit it is making on others.

Did you know...

Although there are many different types of pricing, they can almost all be called 'competitive' pricing. This is because, in any market where there are businesses competing to sell rival products, the price range of products of similar quality is likely to be fairly narrow.

Summary

- Price has to be set within a reasonable range – the amounts people are willing to pay
- This will change according to the product and its stage in the life cycle
- The most important type of pricing is still cost-plus, as costs must be covered
- Businesses can use special pricing strategies to help them grow
- Larger businesses can afford to make short-term losses on products, so are better able to use different pricing strategies

Core knowledge

Most prices are, to some degree, consumer-led and need to be in a particular price range before purchase is even considered. A diamond ring priced at £2.50 would find few takers – consumers would be convinced that it was not worth it. One priced at £25,000 would be out of the price range of most consumers. A ring in the price range of £250 to £2,500 is much more likely to fall within most people's idea of what such a ring should cost.

The most important form of pricing is cost-plus pricing, as this is intended to deliver a profit to the business. You will remember that this is where the business tries to set a price that will cover its costs and allow it to make a profit. To do this it needs to add up all the costs to make a product and then add a mark-up – an extra amount that represents the profit on each product.

Businesses can use different pricing strategies in order to grow. Most pricing strategies may be considered as either short-term promotional prices or different types of competitive pricing that are used at different stages of the product life cycle (see Chapter 7).

There are a number of factors that influence pricing strategy decisions, such as the type of market in which the business operates and the amount of competition in the market. Some markets have high start-up costs or need special machinery or technology. Smaller businesses might therefore find it difficult to enter such markets. Oil and power companies are a good example. Other markets may be highly competitive and easy to enter (certain types of high-street shops, for instance) but also, of course, much easier to exit.

And more

In some markets, the business may have little or no say in the price that it can charge for a product. In a market with many competing businesses all facing similar costs, if any one business tries to raise prices, it is likely to lose a lot of its custom. Customers faced with a lower priced competitor will switch to it in order to save money (providing quality is seen as being equal). In such competitive markets, cost structures usually mean that businesses do not have the option of lowering prices, except in the short term to try to gain market share. Businesses therefore have to accept the market price and are called price takers. They can still compete – but through other elements of the marketing mix rather than price. If there is a leading business in a competitive market, it may decide to use predator or **destroyer pricing**. This is where a business undercuts competitors with the intention of driving them out of business. Sometimes this backfires – the winner is the one that can stand the losses in revenue the longest.

Not all markets, however, have many equal-sized businesses in competition. In some markets there is one dominant business and a number of smaller rivals. In this case, the dominant business may be a price leader or what is called a '**price maker**'. This means that whatever price it charges, all other businesses are forced to follow suit. For example, Brazil produces so much of the world's coffee that it decides on the world price. It can force prices up by restricting supply or down by releasing more of the commodity on to the market. Other businesses in the market have no choice but to accept this price and are called **price takers**.

Brazil's coffee industry is a 'price maker'

Did you know...

Sometimes businesses can charge different prices for the same product because they are selling it in different markets. This works as long as the different markets can be kept separate. Different train fares for different times of the day, or bought in advance or on the day, or online or in person, are all examples.

Have a go!

Group activity

In your group, decide on a commercial TV channel for each of you to watch for one evening. Make a record of each product that is advertised and the pricing strategy that you think is being used. Put these all together and decide which are the most commonly used strategies and why.

Discussion

Businesses with a larger market share may be able to price smaller competitors out of business. These businesses would say that they were more efficient, so the customer is getting a better deal. Customers, however, may think they are being denied choice. What do you think?

Web-based activity

Find 8–10 new products that are currently being launched. 'I Want One of Those' at **www.iwantoneofthose.com** could be a good place to start. Now look at the prices that are being charged for each of them. Draw up a table to show which price strategies you think are being used.

Quickfire questions

1 Name one pricing strategy that could be used for an expensive product.
2 Name one pricing strategy that could be used to enter a market.
3 Name one pricing strategy more likely to be available to a larger business than a small one.
4 Outline what is meant by a 'price range'.
5 Outline what is meant by 'cost-plus' pricing.
6 What sort of products in general are launched with prices that skim the market?
7 What is a loss leader? Why is it used?
8 What is a premium price? Why is it used?
9 What is a penetration price? Why is it used?
10 Outline how market dominance is linked to price.

Hit the spot

> Outline three possible factors that might influence pricing strategy decisions.

> Explain the difference between a 'price maker' and a 'price taker'.

> What is competitive pricing? Explain, with reasons, whether it is true to say that most prices may be defined as competitive.

Cracking the code

Destroyer pricing Where a business charges a low price to drive rivals out of business.

Loss leaders Products priced at a low price that does not cover cost to attract customers to the business.

Market share The slice of a market that each business has – usually measured as a percentage.

Penetration price Price set below those of competitors so that a business can gain a share in a market.

Premium pricing When prices are set at a high level to try to emphasise the quality of the product.

Price maker When one business dominates a market, it can dictate price.

Price takers Businesses in a competitive market, or small businesses in a market dominated by a price maker.

Skimming An initial high price, aimed to 'skim the cream' off the market.

Chapter 9
The marketing mix: promotion

IN THE NEWS

It is not just businesses that want to grow. Sometimes governments encourage business growth by providing the framework and facilities for businesses. Sponsorship, product endorsements and the use of famous names and brands can be key factors in the success of a product or project.

In the case of Dubai Sports City, the product is the first purpose-built sports city in the world. The promoters were keen to attract businesses, suppliers and customers, so have made use of some of the biggest names in sport to promote their $2 billion investment. The investors have gone for top-name sponsorship – Manchester United will host the football academy, with their own branded Manchester United Soccer School, and football (along with rugby and athletics) will take place in a new 60,000-seat stadium. The football academy is being established with the help of United's commercial partner, Nike. Top international golfer Ernie Els has designed the championship golf course, The Dunes, which is at the centre of a residential development. The golf academy will be run by another top player, Butch Harmon, while former international tennis star David Lloyd will lend his name to the tennis academy and Rodney Marsh, Test cricketer and former director of the England and Wales Cricket Board National Academy, will run the world's first global cricket academy.

Of course, it is not just a sports city but a community, including schools, hospitals, leisure opportunities, residences and shops. At the heart of it there will be a sports-themed retail mall of around 1.2 million square feet. The big names will help to draw in retailers, leisure providers and the public, allowing businesses already based in Dubai to grow on the back of this promotion, or encourage new businesses to establish. While sponsorship and product endorsements are 'below-the-line', this does not stop them being just as powerful as the 'above-the-line' spending.

The first stage of the complex opened in 2007 and it is due for completion in 2010.

 You can see a promotional video for Dubai Sports City at **www.youtube.com/ watch?v=0cOavxxiMxo**. List the key business messages that the promotion is

Purpose of promotion

Dubai knows that its use of famous names and leading brands will attract businesses to its development. These, in turn, will attract customers using their own **promotional strategies**. Promotion serves two main purposes: to inform the customer of the existence of a product and to persuade them to buy it. Promotion can therefore be a major tool in helping a business to grow. It will be used not only to help boost sales but also to increase market share.

> ## Did you know...
>
> Promotion may be to the consumer, but may also be directly to the trade to encourage suppliers to push products through the distribution system (see Chapter 10). Such promotion is often at specialist trade fairs and exhibitions aimed at businesses.

How being bigger helps

As a business grows it is likely to have a bigger budget for advertising and promotional activities. It may also be able to concentrate on particular products if it has a wider product portfolio (see Chapter 7) and target promotion on those products that are likely to be more profitable.

Promotion is used to help a business grow by encouraging more sales and a bigger market share. All promotional activities come with a cost – advertising, promotional prices and all **above-the-line** activities come at a price. Businesses must carefully budget and be aware of whether promotion is being effective not just in terms of sales but in terms of what it is costing to gain those sales.

Above and below

Any promotional activity (such as advertising) that is paid for directly is called 'above-the-line'

promotional expenditure. Other methods of promotion are called **'below-the-line'** expenditure. Much below-the-line promotion is public relations (PR). PR is used to bring a product or brand to the attention of the public without using direct advertising. It includes areas such as celebrity endorsement of products, sponsorship and creating 'news' items around products. It is, for example, worth paying a 'celebrity' to open a new facility, providing there is plenty of publicity to go with the event. Sponsorship is also used to link a product to its positive benefits, e.g. performance oils and motor racing, and sometimes just to keep a name in the public eye, for example, the Emirates Stadium, the Carling Cup. PR agencies will arrange newsworthy 'photo opportunities', interviews and other publicity, such as book signings or product placement in films or magazines. **Corporate hospitality** is another PR growth area. A business will buy tickets for a sporting or other event and use them to 'reward' clients to encourage loyalty and repeat business.

A growing business will use sales promotion and special promotional prices. Short-term price cuts such as sale prices, competitions and 'added-value' promotions (money off, Buy One Get One Free, etc.) are all used to boost sales, market share and customer loyalty.

The Carling Cup

Advertising

Advertising – above-the-line – spending tends to be expensive, but can also be effective. The more effective it is, the more it will cost. TV advertising reaches millions and is therefore very expensive. However, businesses can cut down costs by trying to target particular groups. Direct marketing targets likely customers through mailshots or, increasingly, by using new technology. E-mails, texts and automated phone calls are all popular now.

Influence of markets

The choice of promotional method will be influenced by the nature of the product and the market in which it is being sold. For example, a specialist product will target advertising at its specialist market. Some products are so specialist (and often so expensive) that they are usually sold through agents advertising in specialist publications or on websites. Examples include industrial machinery, plant and equipment.

Businesses may also respond to competitor promotions with promotions of their own. Often a successful campaign by one business in a market will be followed by a counter-campaign by another, intent on gaining back its market share.

Summary

- Promotion has two main purposes – information and persuasion
- Growing businesses will have the opportunity for larger promotional budgets
- Bigger businesses must still make sure that promotion is effective
- Promotion is either paid for directly (above-the-line) or is indirect (below-the-line)
- The choice of promotion is linked to the type of product and type and size of market
- Direct marketing can cut down promotional costs and reach specific target groups

Core knowledge

Promotion needs to tell customers and potential customers about the existence and benefits of a product. The main way to achieve this is through advertising, with its aim summed up by the acronym **AIDA**. Advertising should attract Attention, create Interest, develop Desire and lead to Action. It should highlight the positive features of a product that will attract customers – price, performance, variety, etc. – depending on the product and market. Promotion should highlight the USP (unique selling point) – this is the single aspect that makes this product better than any of the competition.

Good timing is vital. The business needs to make sure that products are available to coincide with promotion, to cope with increased demand. If they are not and there are shortages, this could make the advertising counter-productive. There are key 'moments' when certain advertising is most effective. For instance, it is immediately after Christmas, in the dark days of January, that people are persuaded to cheer themselves up by booking a summer holiday, whereas before Christmas toys and games will be advertised much more heavily (and prices will stay high).

The media mix chosen to promote a product must be linked closely to the target market, the budget for promotion and the product itself.

Promotion is all about passing on a message (about a product) to a customer through the appropriate media. Media just means the way in which the message is carried. Advertising media include broadcast media, such as television and cinema advertisements – these are expensive to make and broadcast but highly effective, reaching a wide audience. Radio advertisements are much cheaper to make and to broadcast, but surprisingly effective. Print media (catalogues, leaflets, magazines, newspapers) can be colourful and contain additional detailed information. They can also encourage instant customer response through reply or order forms. Posters and billboards are also classed as print media. A national poster campaign can be highly effective, but will also be expensive.

Did you know...

A successful brand is worth its weight in gold. The message of a good brand can achieve all the parts of AIDA on its own. A brand image can attract attention, is heavily linked to the image of the business or product, is desirable and will encourage people to buy products with that brand instead of other products.

And more

Advertising media become more expensive as they become more effective. So TV advertising or national poster campaigns are the most expensive of all. Some advertising can be fairly precisely targeted using particular broadcast times, particular TV and radio programmes, specialist magazines and journals and even postcode areas. Other promotions, such as poster advertising, will just aim to reach as many people as possible and hit the target market in this way. Businesses need to try to choose the right media to ensure that the message is being delivered to the correct market segment. Delivering a powerful and persuasive message, but to the wrong market segment, is a waste of time and promotional budget. Promotional budgets have to be carefully spent to achieve a balance between three different aims: coverage, penetration and cost.

- Coverage refers to the number of people reached – poster advertisements have very high coverage but reach many more than the intended target market.
- Penetration refers to how much of a particular market the promotion reaches. For example, a print advertisement in a popular specialist magazine (such as one linked to a sport or hobby) is likely to have high penetration of that market. If you are going to advertise football boots, advertise them in a football magazine, not a gardening one! Advertising costs for print media are linked to circulation, with figures and costs published each year in *BRAD* (*British Rate and Data*). There are hundreds of specialist publications that can be targeted.
- Cost must include two elements – the making or design and the distribution or broadcast costs. Most expensive is TV advertising, both to make and to broadcast. At the opposite end of the scale, leaflets can be cheap to produce and distribute, but still be highly effective in reaching a target market.

Did you know...

Product placement can extend to some very high-cost items. In some action movies, cars and even helicopters may be provided for free by the manufacturer. The resulting publicity from a successful film would have cost much, much more to buy.

Have a go!

Group activity

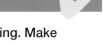

In your group, decide on a commercial TV channel for each of you to watch for one evening. Make a record of each product that is advertised and note the group at which you think it is targeted. Suggest how each advertisement could be rewritten to target a different group.

Discussion

Advertising, whether by TV, radio, poster, magazine or even point-of-sale, is all a waste of resources that could be better used on making more products. Advertising contributes nothing to business but does cost a lot of money. Do you think this is true? Should all advertising be banned?

Web-based activity

Visit **www.brandchannel.com/brandcameo_films.asp** where you can see which brands have been featured in recent movies. Choose three of these and explain for each what it is you think the product manufacturers were hoping to gain from that particular film.

Quickfire questions

1   Give the two reasons for promotion.
2   What is 'above-the-line' promotion?
3   What is 'below-the-line' promotion?
4   Give an example of 'below-the-line' promotion.
5   What is meant by 'corporate hospitality'?
6   Give an example of a short-term sales promotion.
7   Give an example of how a business could target particular groups through promotions.
8   What does AIDA stand for?
9   What is a USP?
10 Give two reasons why some media are more expensive than others.

Hit the spot

> Describe how the growth of a business might help it in terms of promotion.

>> Explain why a promotional campaign in a particular market is often followed by another campaign in the same market.

>>> Outline three of the promotional strategies being used by Dubai Sports City. Explain which you think will be most effective and why.

Cracking the code

Above-the-line Promotional activity, such as advertising, that is paid for directly.

Aida Used as a reminder that advertising should attract Attention, create Interest, develop Desire and lead to Action

Below-the-line Promotional activity that is not directly paid-for advertising expenditure.

Corporate hospitality When a business provides 'gifts' for its clients as a reward for their loyalty. These can include free bars, tickets to events and seats at shows and concerts.

Promotional strategies The various 'mixes' of different promotions used by businesses.

Chapter 10
The marketing mix: place

IN THE NEWS

The 2008 Christmas charts were dominated by two versions of Leonard Cohen's ballad 'Hallelujah', with over half a million downloads. X Factor winner Alexandra Burke hit number one, selling 576,000 copies on CD and via downloads. Jeff Buckley's version, which fans claim is better than Burke's, reached number two – remarkably, on download sales alone. The charts have become vital to the music industry, but it was not until 1952 that enough recorded music was sold in order to make a chart possible. The very first number 1 (Al Martino's 'Here in My Heart') was in November of that year. Since then, popular music has had a habit of reinventing itself to take advantage of the latest technology. First, single records, then EPs and LPs (Extended Play records and Long Playing albums), tapes and cassettes. Later CDs were used for better-quality digital sound.

More recently, recorded music has found a whole new way of being distributed. Traditionally, sounds were recorded on disk or some other form of hard media, sent into shops, bought and played on home systems. Now, all that has changed and the physical distribution of recorded music is no longer the main way by which music is distributed. The medium of choice for playing music is now a portable digital player, or even a mobile phone – 60% of digital tracks are downloaded to computer devices, 40% to mobile phones. The means of buying music, led by iTunes but with many more websites following, is by internet download. There are now more than 500 legitimate digital music services worldwide, offering over 6 million tracks, with single-track downloads rapidly approaching 2 billion a year. (Around 20 times the amount bought have been swapped via illegal file-sharing sites.)

Once downloads were counted in the charts alongside physical sales, they were always bound to increase. Just after Christmas 2005, an important milestone was reached with the download of over 1 million digital tracks in a single week and by the end of 2008, downloads accounted for more than 15% of record companies' revenue, up from 0% in 2004, and in America, the main digital market, over 30%. In the same period, CD sales fell by around 10%. Chairman of IFPI (the International Federation of the Phonographic Industry) John Kennedy commented: 'A new wave of digital commerce, from mobile to broadband, is rolling out across the world. It is generating billions of dollars and being driven to a large extent by music' (*IFPI Annual Digital Music Report,* January 2006).

@ You will find the report 'Internet shopping – an OFT (Office of Fair Trading) market study' at **www.oft.gov.uk/ shared_oft/reports/consumer_ protection/oft921.pdf**
In the summary of the report there are four bullet points that outline some of the problems of online trade. Suggest possible solutions for each.

Internet sales

How do you buy your music? Is it 'physical' – through a high-street outlet or traditional record store – or is it digital – via a legal music site? It is not just music, however, that is taking advantage of low-cost distribution. The value of all goods sold over the internet continues to increase at a rapid rate. The most recent UK government figures are for 2005, when there was £21 billion worth of sales made by over 20 million UK adults, over half of whom spent over £500. These UK Office for National Statistics figures also state that at least 62,000 UK businesses were selling online. Online spending increased by 76% between 2006 and 2007, in figures taken from www.sitemakers.co.uk that put spending at £53.3 billion.

The most popular purchases are travel and holidays, with electricals, clothing and groceries rapidly catching up. The spread of high-speed broadband, and its improved reliability, has been one of the major factors in the increase in online shopping. The size of a business does not affect the ability of that business to put up a website and take orders, but will affect the number of product lines it can reliably offer for sale and may also affect its ability to deliver an effective service.

According to the OFT, people shop online because they find it convenient, it increases choice and helps them find lower prices. Retailers sell online to reach more customers, to sell 24/7 and to compete with rivals.

Did you know...

Major retail outlets that offered internet sales early have built up a strong customer base. Tesco, the grocery chain, is the fourth largest UK internet retailer behind Amazon, Dell and Argos. Amazon is an internet-only retailer, with huge warehouses and a sophisticated distribution system, Dell decided as early as 1996 to offer an online service, to cut out the 'middle man' and pass the savings on to the customer, while Argos found it easy to transfer its catalogue-based experience onto the web.

Different channels of distribution

Place is not just the place where you can buy the product but how the product is delivered to the consumer. As you learned in Unit 1, Setting up a Business, different **distribution channels** are used depending on the product (does it need to get there quickly, safely?) and the market (size and location). Traditional **long-chain distribution** passes from the manufacturer through wholesaler to retail outlets. Each 'link' is called an **intermediary**. Businesses can either push products out to intermediaries or rely on consumer demand pulling the products through the distribution chain. To push products down the chain, a business can offer incentives to intermediaries. This applies to any business in the chain pushing to the next one, a wholesaler to a retailer, for example. Pull strategy involves using promotion to increase customer demand.

Wholesalers and retailers then have to order more products to meet demand.

The shortest distribution chain is directly to the consumer. Businesses can look for sales through direct approaches such as e-mail and telephone sales and a small number of products may still be sold door-to-door. There is also still a fairly large market for mail-order goods, via catalogues, although this is rapidly being replaced with internet sales.

Why customers choose

Customers choose retail outlets according to a number of factors which include:

● convenience – the act of buying a product needs to be easy; this includes ease of ordering, having different methods of payment available and home delivery if necessary;

- cost – if the cost of distribution, or to get to a retail outlet, outweighs the benefit from the product, then the customer will not buy. Amazon would sell a lot fewer books if people had to go to a shop rather than order online;

- reliability – customers want to know that products will be available when they want, at the stated prices;

- value added – this includes areas like low-cost credit, after-sales service and competitive pricing.

A high street site could also be high cost

Why businesses choose

The key factors when a business is choosing 'place' include:

- cost – expensive sites or networks have to 'earn their keep' in sales;

- available distribution channels – if there are competing channels from which to choose, this can keep costs down;

- margins – lower costs and higher revenues lead to greater profit margins.

Summary

- Place refers to both where a product is bought and how it gets there – distribution
- It is an important part of the marketing mix
- The correct 'place' depends on the type of product and the market that it is in
- Distribution is changing as new channels, such as the internet, become available
- This means channels can be shortened, even to the shortest distribution channel – direct from producer to consumer
- Customers' choice of 'place' is influenced by convenience, cost, reliability and value added
- Businesses' choice of 'place' is influenced by cost, distribution channels and margins

Core knowledge

The distribution of a product refers both to the place where it may be bought and to the means by which it is delivered to that place. The traditional places for retail transactions are shops; other outlets and methods have also been developed as businesses seek better ways to compete. A growing business will have the choice of more distribution channels and will be able to carry a greater variety of stock. Shops range from department store to small convenience stores, including multiple chains selling goods or services such as WH Smith selling books and stationery or KwikFit selling car services. Other outlets include vending machines, catalogues and direct sales.

Many small retailers survive by offering a specialist or personalised service (e.g. haircutting) or value added in other ways, such as convenience or personal service. Much retail trade now takes place via mail order or the internet. This, too, has revolutionised retailing, so that many shops have felt that they need an internet presence alongside their high-street one. These are called 'bricks and clicks' retailers, while increasingly many have done away with (or never had) the 'bricks' element. In some cases, such as with expensive items like industrial machinery or houses, sales are direct or through an agent, although even here online elements are possible.

Consumers will choose outlets according to convenience, cost, reliability and value added, producers according to cost, distribution channels and the profit margins they can earn (see Chapter 40). Being the leading or largest business in a market is important. Smaller outlets that have room to stock only a limited amount of a product will prefer to stock the market leading product and other products may be 'frozen out'.

And more

Place is just one part of the marketing mix, but an important one, that needs a whole range of specialised transport and storage services. Distribution is the way in which the product travels from the producer to the consumer (sometimes via an outlet, but not always). The business branch that deals with transport, delivery and the management of the entire supply chain from producer to consumer is called logistics. The channel of distribution chosen and amount and type of storage necessary depend on a number of factors. Some products must be delivered fresh; some are bulky and expensive to store; some require refrigeration, or security, or other special treatment.

Traditional 'long-channel' distribution passes along a chain from producer to manufacturer via wholesaler and retailer to the final consumer. Any channel which succeeds in cutting out one or more of these stages is called short-channel distribution and, in general, is cheaper than long-channel distribution. Typically, the shorter the distribution channel, the lower the costs involved. So, for example, Amazon's postal deliveries of books and DVDs and Dell's direct delivery to customers is cheaper than using intermediaries. Intermediaries are the 'middle men' (or women) who provide a service to the people before and after them in the chain of distribution. The major intermediaries are:

● wholesalers, who provide storage (including special storage such as refrigerated or secure units) and 'break bulk'. This means that they buy in large amounts ('bulk', e.g. by the lorry load) and sell on in smaller amounts (e.g. by the case);

● merchants, who buy goods at a price with the intention of selling them on at a higher price; and

● agents, who buy and sell products on behalf of both customers and businesses (such as estate agents selling houses for owners).

Did you know...

Many businesses prefer to have their own stock and distribution systems and have developed their own warehouses and logistics to ensure that they have what they want when they need it. In a number of cases, this has given them such market power that they can pressurise producers for lower prices.

Did you know...

Stockless distribution is a version of the 'just-in-time' production method. Stock is timed to arrive at a retail outlet exactly when it is needed in a continuous cycle of sales and re-stocking. This means lower costs. It also means that fresh produce really is fresh.

Transport is just one part of 'place' – distributing product

Have a go!

Group activity

Carry out a survey in your group to find out how much is now bought online rather than at shops. Each person should write down the last ten things that they bought and say whether it was online or at a retail outlet. What sort of patterns emerge? What sort of reasons can people give for using one method or another?

Discussion

The growth of chains has been blamed for making all high streets look the same, while the growth of some retail giants (supermarkets in particular) has been blamed for the decline of small local shops and specialists. Others say that chains and supermarkets bring more reliability and lower prices. What do you think?

Web-based activity

Go to **www.bbc.co.uk/radio1/chart/singles.shtml** and look at the official charts, then go to **www.bbc.co.uk/radio1/chart/downloads.shtml** for the downloads chart. Are they the same or different? Explain why you think this is so. (You should refer to different parts of the market.)

Quickfire questions

1 Outline the two parts to 'place' in the marketing mix.
2 What are the most popular online purchases?
3 Outline the stages in long-chain distribution.
4 What is the shortest possible chain of distribution?
5 Name three traditional places for retail transactions.
6 What is meant by 'logistics'?
7 Suggest three ways by which products can be sold directly.
8 Suggest two areas where a retailer could add value for a consumer.
9 Suggest two ways by which a retailer can make the act of purchasing more convenient.
10 Give the two factors that affect the profit margins of a business.

Hit the spot

> Give two reasons why internet sales have increased so rapidly.

> Explain the difference between 'push' and 'pull' strategies in the distribution chain.

> Explain the reasons why both consumers and retailers are keen to trade online. Which do you think is the most important reason for each and why?

Cracking the code

Distribution channels The ways by which products reach the final consumer.

Intermediary Any person or organisation that provides a 'link', such as agents, wholesalers, retailers.

Long-chain distribution When a product passes through every intermediary from manufacturer to consumer.

FINANCE FOR A LARGE BUSINESS

Chapter 11
Introduction to finance for a large business

In this section

Introduction to finance for a large business
Sources of finance for a large business
Profit and loss accounts
Balance sheets
Ratios

The finance function is central to all businesses, large and small. Businesses need finance with which to start up, with which to buy stock, premises, equipment, marketing and advertising materials. This must not only be found – from sources as varied as private investors, venture capitalists, pension funds, banks, governments, property, local authorities, etc. – but also managed. Someone has to be in charge of knowing what money is flowing into the business and what is leaving it, and at what rate. While a small business may have its finance managed by its owner, or may employ a specialist accounting firm, in many larger businesses financial management will be carried out by a separate department within the business. The people in the finance or accounting department will be responsible for managing flows of money and for ensuring that all other parts of the business receive sufficient funds as and when they need them. They will also keep accurate records of such flows and be able to provide these to stakeholders and external bodies which have a right to see them, for example, shareholders and the tax authorities.

Although some sources are available to both large and small businesses, in general large businesses have different ways of raising finance to small businesses. They might have profits made from past transactions that they can re-invest in the business, they might be able to issue shares on the stock exchange, or sell more shares to existing shareholders, they might be able to sell equipment, buildings, factories, transport – even processes and brand names – that they no longer need. They can also use those things that they own – assets – as security for further loans.

You need a good head for figures to keep track of all this

Financial records

The financial records of the business are kept in its yearly accounts. For small businesses, these are for the benefit of the owners and may also be used by the tax authorities to work out how much tax is owed. Larger businesses have a wider range of people to whom their accounts might be important. Public limited companies, in particular, have a legal duty to publish their annual accounts and to make them available to the general public as well as their own shareholders and the tax authorities. People with an interest in the performance of the business (stakeholders) can then use these accounts to assess how well the business is performing. A large business may produce monthly, weekly or even day-to-day accounts and may also produce separate sets of accounts for different parts of the business. These may be divided up geographically or by product, so that the business can see the costs (and contribution to profits) of different parts of the business.

Cost accounting

A key part of the management of finance is cost accounting. These are the detailed records of costs kept by the business to help it keep track of its expenditure. Cost accounting is complicated by there being so many different types of cost. It is up to the financial managers in the business to decide how each cost is defined. For example, costs may be:

● *direct or indirect*. Direct costs are those that are paid as a result of the production of a good or service. They will therefore include raw materials, components and parts and labour. These are also called variable costs, as they vary with production. Indirect costs are those that are not directly linked to production but which are essential to it, such as heating and lighting, power, rent, rates and even part of the costs of labour (such as management costs). These are also called fixed costs as they do not change as production changes;

● *set-up or running costs*. Some costs have to be paid only once, when the business is established – others have to be paid to keep the business going.

Types of accountant

The accountants that create and use the accounts of a business are divided into two groups – management accounting and financial accounting. Financial accountants are those who create the formal accounts of the business to show how it has performed over a certain time period, usually the previous year. These are prepared in order to comply with legal requirements and can allow the business to review its progress against previous years or against competitors in the same time period.

The 1985 Companies Act requires large companies to publish a balance sheet, a profit and loss account and a cash flow statement. Essentially, these are accounts that look at, and record, the past performance of a business. They show the importance of profit and loss accounts, the balance sheet and records of cash flows into and out of the business. By contrast, management accounts are drawn up for internal use. Management accounting is the production of accounts and figures that forecast the future performance of the business and which can

Figures can be used to make forecasts

therefore be used to make predictions and to manage the business. This type of account includes cash flow forecasts (the *forecast* looks to the future, the *statement* looks to the past).

The main types of account

You will need to understand the main types of account and some of the key tools that are available to accountants and managers to judge how well a business is doing. The accounts that are most important are the profit and loss account and the balance sheet. From these two sets of figures, a business can work out its gross and net profit and see how well it is performing in its market. It can also measure how profitable it is and how efficient it is by using ratios – these will show it, for instance, which products are most profitable and which resources are being

used most efficiently. This will enable the business to plan production, marketing and other activities in the next time period.

Two important factors for a business are therefore the accuracy and thoroughness of financial figures and records and the ability to interpret these figures in order to make decisions.

Changes

It is also worth remembering that this part of business, like all other parts, is constantly changing. To make accounts clearer, plcs are being asked to use different terms for some parts of their accounts and smaller businesses will have to follow suit. Keep a look out for these new terms, which may, for a while, appear alongside the current ones.

Chapter 12
Sources of finance for a large business

IN THE NEWS

In the autumn of 2008, many large businesses found themselves under pressure due to falling order books as growth in the economy slowed. Some big businesses, in particular banks and other financial institutions, found themselves in deep trouble and short of funds. They therefore took a traditional route to raising funds and asked shareholders for more money. Halifax Bank of Scotland (HBOS) asked its investors for a further £4 billion. Raising funds in this way is called a 'rights' issue. This is because existing shareholders are given the right to buy the new shares. The issue was announced on 29 April 2008, with the new shares priced at 275p – almost half the price of its shares at the time, which stood at 500p. But a lack of confidence in the bank led shareholders to take up few of the shares on offer. Just 124 million shares – less than 9% of the number on offer – were bought, leaving the underwriters (businesses that had promised to buy the few shares they thought would remain) with 1,375 billion shares, or almost £3.8 billion worth.

In the week before the offer, shares in HBOS had fallen to as low as 225p. This meant that it was cheaper for investors to buy existing shares in the market than the new issue – if they were persuaded to buy at all! Although the price rose to 282p, this was too late to persuade investors to change their minds.

Usually such a 'cash call' (as this is known) would be successful and a good way for a large business to raise additional finance. In this case,

however, confidence in the banking system – and the fall in the share price of HBOS – left it to fail. Money was still raised – but not as much as had been hoped – and most of the shares stayed in the hands of the merchant banks that were the underwriters for the issue, rather than with small investors. The two investment banks that were the underwriters tried to sell some of the shares in the market, but were still left with over 1 billion shares each.

Go to **www.guardian.co.uk/ business/2008/jul/22/ hbosbusiness.banking1** where you can read about the rights issue. Links from this page will take you to other examples of rights issues and frequently asked questions about rights.

More sources of finance

Some sources of finance are from within the business. These are called internal sources. Some, called external sources, are from outside the business.

External sources

- *Share capital*. A business which changes its ownership from, for example, a partnership or private limited company to a public limited company does so in order to raise finance via the stock exchange. It offers shares for sale to investors. This is called '**floating**' a company. After it has been floated, or if it needs to raise more money, it can issue new shares. These can be offered for sale to everyone or just to its existing shareholders. If a business decides to issue extra shares in order to raise more money, investors run the risk of losing their money if things do not go well. For the business, it means that there are more people or organisations with an interest in the business, so existing owners and directors could lose some of their power.

- ***Venture capital***. Some entrepreneurs are happy to take a risk on a new business so will provide investment. They are likely to want a share in the running of the business and certainly a share in its profits, should it make any. Such investments are generally in higher-risk businesses such as, for example, those developing new technology. However, the benefit to the entrepreneur is that they are also businesses that have a chance of making high profits. For the business, the advantage may come in having the expertise of the entrepreneur and his or her business connections, and that such investments are

not loans, so do not carry interest. The downside is that current owners will have to lose some control over the business and share their profits.

- *Loans*. Banks and other financial institutions may agree to lend money to a business. They will want to be sure that the money will be repaid. Often this means that they ask for some sort of **security**. This could, for example, be the assets of the business (buildings, factories, vehicles, processes, brands, etc.). In other cases they may want a say in the management of the business. The government also provides a loan-guarantee scheme through the Department of Trade and Industry. Loans may be short, medium or long term and have fixed or variable interest rates. Obtaining the right loan might give a business security and flexibility, but loans can also be costly in terms of interest payments. Banks can also decide that a risk is too great and demand that the loan is returned. This could cause the business to fail.

- *Leasing*. A business can 'rent' assets (such as machinery or vehicles) through a leasing arrangement. It pays a fixed amount per year to hire the assets so gains the use of them without having to pay for the capital.

Internal sources

- ***Retained profits***. An important source of finance for a large business may be its own profits. Profits may be either shared among the shareholders or kept by the business. Profits that are shared are called distributed profits. They are usually shared in the form of a dividend. This means that the profit is divided by the number of shares and each share receives an equal part of it. That kept by the business is called undistributed or retained profit. The main advantage for the business is that this money is not borrowed, so no interest is paid. The main disadvantage may be in shareholders not receiving high dividends.

- *Selling unwanted assets.* If a business has an **asset** (something it owns) that it no longer needs, then it can sell it. Some businesses may move into different markets and no longer need certain assets. For example, a food producer that decided to stop selling frozen food and concentrate on fresh food would no longer need refrigerators and other freezing plant and equipment.

Plant may be sold off if no longer needed

Did you know...

Short-term finance is generally defined as borrowing from a few days up to three years and includes overdrafts, loans, trade credit and hire purchase. Medium-term finance is from three to ten years. Long-term finance is ten years plus and includes term loans and mortgages.

Summary

- When a business grows it may need more sources of finance than a small business
- It will also have access to more sources of finance
- Sources may be internal (from within the business) or external (from outside the business)
- Finance has to be of the appropriate size, risk and time period for the business
- The type of business is therefore important when choosing the type of finance

Core knowledge

Small businesses, you will remember from Section 2: Starting a Business, have limited sources of finance. Most often, the owners use their personal funds to finance the business. Should the business be a success and grow, however, it can then think about other sources of finance. Sources of finance for a large business may be external or internal. Internal finance comes from within the business. The main sources of internal finance for a large business are retained profit and the sale of assets. Retained profit is estimated to provide up to two thirds of the finance of large businesses. But owners' funds also form a key part of the finance of larger businesses. With a limited company, in particular a public limited company, the owners will be the shareholders. To become a public limited company, the business must sell shares on the stock exchange. Once it has done so, it has the option of raising more money from existing shareholders. As the business grows, it is also likely to have much more in the way of assets that can therefore be used as security against loans.

The performance of the business and the size to which it has grown will also be major factors that affect both how the business obtains finance and, perhaps more significantly, the cost of the finance. If a business is seen to be doing well, can report increased sales, bigger markets and better profits, then the value of its shares will increase. This does not raise any more money for the company as the shares have already been sold into the market. It does, however, raise the value of the company, so that lending to it may be more attractive, and gives it the confidence to issue new shares. The cost of a loan may also be lowered by a larger business. If a loan is particularly large or the business is particularly strong, lenders may agree to lower rates of interest or other specialist terms.

And more

Each method of raising funds may have advantages and disadvantages as explained, but will also be more or less suitable depending on the situation. Different businesses, in different situations, will find that one method is more suitable than another. Key factors include the size of the finance, the time period over which it is needed or can be paid back and the cost of the finance.

Some businesses have a very broad asset base – in other words, they need a lot of assets in order to operate. A steel manufacturer, for example, needs plant, equipment, factories and stocks of raw materials so is likely to have many assets that can be used to raise money. Other businesses may have few assets. A business like eBay, for example, is run on the internet and needs little more than office space. It would have to find other ways to raise finance if it wished to expand, as it has no assets to sell or to provide as security.

Sometimes finance can be raised through other flexible and imaginative routes. A common one of these is 'sale and leaseback'. This is where the business still needs the asset but wants to raise money from it. Supermarket giant Tesco, for example, has sold a number of its sites and then leased them back. This means that it no longer owns the asset but still has use of it. The advantage of this is that it raises finance without borrowing. The disadvantage is that the business runs the risk of losing the use of the asset altogether. The business could also mortgage property that it owns (this means raising money with the property as security), again running the risk of losing the asset.

Some Tesco sites were sold and leased back

Did you know...

Underwriters are people who take on risks – often they work for insurance companies. They are called underwriters because, in the old days, as each investor took on a share of a risk, she or he wrote his or her name under the other risk-takers.

Have a go!

Group activity

Use the link **www.guardian.co.uk/business/2008/jul/22/hbosbusiness. banking1** to find out all you can about rights issues. Put together an information leaflet or web page to explain rights issues to someone who has no idea what they are. Remember, you will have to explain all the technical terms that you use as well!

Discussion

Once a business has shareholders, it is possible for the owners to lose some degree of control over the business. Do you think that this is a good or bad thing to happen? What extra benefits do you think that shareholders bring and what problems might they introduce?

Web-based activity

@

Visit **www.bbc.co.uk/celebdaq/** and you can take part in a game that simulates the movement of stocks and shares by letting you buy shares in celebrities rather than companies. Once you sign up you have £10,000 to spend on 'shares' in celebrities, whose price goes up and down (as with real shares) according to their performance. The aim is to make money from dividend payments and from buying and selling shares and the game mirrors how a real stock market works.

Quickfire questions

1   What is a rights issue?
2   What is an underwriter?
3   Why are underwriters called underwriters?
4   Outline the difference between internal and external sources of finance.
5   Give one reason why a larger business has more choice of finance than a smaller one.
6   What does it mean to 'float' a business?
7   What is venture capital?
8   Who sets the main interest rate, to which all others are linked?
9   Which government department provides business loan guarantees?
10 What is the most important source of internal finance?

Hit the spot

> Give two sources of external finance.

>> Explain what is meant by security and why it is important to some lenders.

>>> Judge which you think is the best form of external finance and explain why you think so.

Cracking the code

Asset Something which a business owns.

Floating a company When the company offers shares for sale to the public, via a stock exchange.

Retained profits The profits of the company not distributed in dividends but kept to invest in the business.

Rights issue When existing shareholders are given the right to buy new shares in a business.

Security Property or other assets offered as backing for a loan.

Venture capital Money put up by an entrepreneur willing to take a risk on a new business.

Chapter 13
Profit and loss accounts

IN THE NEWS

Unlike most top football clubs, Arsenal FC is a public limited company. This means that its accounts are published and anyone can see how well it is doing. Arsenal is owned by Arsenal Holdings plc, with the major shareholders being Danny Fiszman, a Swiss-resident diamond dealer with 24.1%, Russian residents Alisher Usmanov and Farhad Moshiri with 24.0%, Lady Nina Bracewell-Smith with 15.9%, US resident Stan Kroenke with 12.4%, and UK-based Richard Carr with 4.3%. The club has two major trading arms – football and property – and is one of the few Premiership clubs that makes a profit, posting £36.7 million profit in the financial year ending 2008. (Chelsea lost £76 million in the same period, Manchester United £58 million and Liverpool £22 million.)

The profit and loss account lets all shareholders – major and minor ones – and all those stakeholders interested in the fortunes of the club (on and off the pitch) know how well it is doing. In the year ended 31 May 2008, Arsenal's revenue was up £23 million on the previous period to £223 million, due to factors such as increased income from selling broadcasting and TV rights and, of course, match-day income from supporters, season ticket holders and corporate clients, which was up to £94.6 million.

The property part of the business is responsible for redeveloping the Highbury site now the club has moved to its new ground at the Emirates Stadium. This did not do as well as expected, although 65 apartments released at the end of July 2008 have raised £18.7 million. The poor performance of the property sector – caused by factors beyond the control of the business – was offset by the higher revenues at the Emirates Stadium since the move. Even though wage costs also went up – by almost a quarter to more than £100 million – the group still managed to make a profit.

A spokesman for Arsenal Holdings plc said that the business had benefited from increased revenue from the new Premier League TV deals and the first Emirates Cup Tournament, which was held in the normally football-free summer months and attracted 110,000 supporters to see Arsenal, Inter Milan, Paris Saint Germain and Valencia compete. Arsenal has also launched its own television channel. Peter Hill-Wood, non-executive chairman, stated in the annual accounts that the figures 'clearly confirm the strength of the Group's financial position following the move to the Emirates Stadium'.

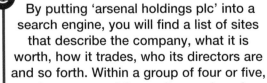

@ By putting 'arsenal holdings plc' into a search engine, you will find a list of sites that describe the company, what it is worth, how it trades, who its directors are and so forth. Within a group of four or five, choose one of these sites each and compare them in terms of the detail they provide. Decide which your group thinks is

Profit and loss account

The **profit and loss account** shows the operational side of the business and whether it is succeeding. It may therefore be divided (as is the case with Arsenal) into different areas. In this way, owners and other stakeholders can see which part of the business is profitable and which

less so. However, in published accounts, the business may not wish to give away this information, so can just publish the global figures. Although the whole thing is generally referred to as the profit and loss account, it actually consists of three parts, only one of which is profit and loss. These three parts are the trading account, the profit and loss account and the appropriation account.

Did you know...

Even the 'quality' of profit may be judged. Profit from continuing good sales of a product (such as Arsenal continuing to perform well in the Premiership) is considered better quality profit than, for example, one-off sales (such as of flats in its property trading arm).

The trading account

The **trading account** shows what products or services have been sold by the business in a specified time period. It shows the income of the business, i.e. what it has earned. For the most part this will be revenue from sales, but some businesses will also have other sources of income. Examples could be interest on investments or loans that have been made, rent from properties or income from patents or licences (another business could pay to use a particular process, for

example). For goods and services sold there are associated costs. These are called the '**cost of sales**' and include items such as raw materials and components. Taking the total cost of sales from total revenue gives the **gross profit**.

This part of the account could look like this: £10,000 worth of **sales revenue** (also called **turnover**). Cost of sales then takes into account that some stock existed at the start of the period (£4000), other stock has been bought (£3000) and some materials have yet to be used (closing stock of £2000).

The trading account

Sales revenue		10000
Minus Cost of sales	opening stock 4000 plus purchases 3000 minus closing stock 2000	5000
Gross profit		5000

The profit and loss account

The middle part of the account is called the profit and loss account. This shows gross profit minus expenses. Gross profit (the final figure on the trading account) is the starting point for this.

Gross profit is the amount that you have made before expenses are taken into account. **Net profit** is the amount after expenses are taken off. Expenses include wages, cost of premises, power, equipment, etc. This part of the account might look like this:

Profit and loss account

Gross profit		5000
Minus Expenses	Rent 500 Wages 500 Transport 200 Power 400 Fuel 200 Equipment 200	2000
Net profit		3000

Did you know...

Many businesses have failed because they have not been able to tell the difference between profit and cash flow. Often a business may think it is doing well because it has full order books and lots of sales, but at the same time its costs may be rising by more than the increase in revenue. This is why it is so important to keep accounts.

The appropriation account

The **appropriation account** shows where the net profit has gone. The starting point for this is net profit (the final figure from the profit and loss account). This account shows what happens to net profit. Some of it goes in taxes, some may be paid to shareholders as dividends, some, as you learned in the previous chapter, may be kept to help finance the business in the future. This is called **retained profit**.

Using the account

The profit and loss account is of use to various groups of stakeholders. It can be used to compare how successful the business was in this trading period compared with the previous one and to see whether it has met its objectives (e.g. Arsenal knows that both revenue and costs have increased, but so has profit). It also helps managers to plan for the future – how can revenue be increased, for example, or costs reduced? In addition, it can help in raising loans from banks, other lenders and investors by showing where costs and revenues arise.

Appropriation account

Net profit		3000
Minus Taxation	1000	
Post-tax profit		2000
Minus Dividends	500	
Retained profit		1500

Summary

- The profit and loss account is used to show the operational side of the business over a set time period
- It can be divided into three parts. These are:
  - the trading account, which shows what the business has earned from sales along with the cost of these sales (cost of sales)
  - the profit and loss account, which shows the effect of expenses on the gross profit figure
  - the appropriation account, which shows how any net profit has been distributed
- The account is useful to various stakeholder groups who can use the figures to assess the performance of the business against similar businesses and in previous time periods

Core knowledge

The profit and loss account is just one of the sets of financial figures that are used by larger businesses. It shows the income of the business from trading and from other activities. For most businesses, the biggest slice of income comes from sales. The number of products sold times the price of those products is the sales revenue. For such sales to take place, however, there must be some associated costs. You may have a mini-enterprise and sell a service such as car washing. In order to sell the service, you would need sponges, wash leathers and detergent. These are the cost of sales. For many businesses, these are the raw materials or components that are used to make the product.

There are also other expenses – for your mini-enterprise, these could be your time and effort, the cost of renting a space on a garage forecourt or the cost of advertising your service. For a large business, expenses include wages, power and equipment costs. What is left is net profit. This is then subject to taxation (it is the income of the business) and what is left can then be distributed to owners or retained for further investment in the business.

In our example, you may want to keep the money for yourself or set up a second site and use the money for this. In a larger business, the same choice – distribute the money to investors or plough it back into the business – is faced. The profit and loss account is an important tool for the stakeholders of the business when assessing the performance of a business. They can see how well sales are doing, which are the most important costs and whether they are rising or falling. Managers and owners can use the figures to make decisions about expansion, prices, costs and the distribution of profits.

And more

Profitability is often the main consideration for stakeholders. A profitable company usually means that the value of shares (and therefore of shareholder holdings) increases, and also gives shareholders the possibility of dividends. Suppliers and other creditors will want to be able to supply with confidence, and profitability is a good indicator of whether or not they will be paid. Taxation authorities such as the Inland Revenue in the UK will be keen to know about company profit so that they can tax the income of the business. Potential investors and lenders, such as entrepreneurs, venture capitalists and banks, will use the account to assess possible risk and reward in the future. It is often, therefore, a useful tool when a business is seeking extra finance from lenders. The main disadvantage of the profit and loss account, however, is that it is always looking backwards at what has happened previously. This means that stakeholders are using past performance in order to judge the likely future performance of a business and this may not always be accurate.

There is also the question of what profit means to a large business. Even in our simplified account above, there are four types of profit. Gross profit is the figure with just cost of sales taken out, net profit (also sometimes termed operating profit) also takes account of expenses and overheads (or fixed costs), while the most important figure for many stakeholders is net profit after taxation, as this shows exactly what is available for distribution to investors, or to provide extra investment for the business to fuel future efficiency (perhaps through new technology or processes) which would improve profitability, or for growth or expansion. If profit is ploughed back into the business, rather than being distributed, it is then termed retained profit.

Did you know...

As this book was being printed, new accounting terms and standards were being introduced to comply with international rules. Exam boards will, for a time, use both, with the new terms in brackets after the old terms. (See Appendix.)

Have a go!

Group activity

List all the different types of profit that you can think of in your group. Each person in the group should then take the role of one stakeholder group and say why the profit and loss account is of particular importance to that group.

Discussion

The law requires companies to produce profit and loss accounts to certain standards and at regular intervals. Why do you think that such accounts have to be made public? Do you think that it is fair that company income should be revealed to everyone in this way?

Web-based activity

Look at the other clubs in the football Premiership and find out which are publicly quoted. Look at the profit and loss accounts for each (go to the 'corporate' or 'investors' part of the website) and decide which is the most profitable. Make sure you follow the rules for making comparisons. If you are not interested in football, you could compare businesses in another sector, fashion for example, or technology.

Quickfire questions

1   What is a public limited company?
2   What is meant by 'sales revenue'?
3   Name three other sources of income, besides sales revenue.
4   Define gross profit.
5   Define net profit.
6   Name the three parts of the profit and loss account.
7   Explain what happens to retained profit.
8   Outline the usual items included in cost of sales.
9   Explain what is meant by 'dividends'.
10 Give one major limitation to the usefulness of profit and loss accounts.

Hit the spot

> Draw up an imaginary profit and loss account for a company of your choice. Label each part and add definitions.

> Give three stakeholder groups for whom profit is important and say why.

> Explain how you can be sure that you are comparing like with like when looking at different businesses and why this is important.

Cracking the code

Appropriation account This shows where the net profit has been distributed.

Cost of sales The cost of items such as raw materials and components used to make goods or provide services.

Gross profit Sales revenue minus cost of sales.

Net profit The amount after expenses are taken off gross profit.

Profit and loss account The account that shows the operational side of the business.

Retained profit Profit that is kept to help finance the business in the future.

Sales revenue Product sold times price.

Trading account The part of the profit and loss account that shows the income of the business, i.e. what it has earned.

Turnover Another way of saying 'sales revenue'.

Chapter 14
Balance sheets

During the late summer and early autumn of 2008, as stock markets fell and unemployment began to rise, a number of financial institutions found themselves under pressure. All banks and building societies that accept deposits rely on the confidence of those who have trusted money to them. If that confidence ever slips, this causes what is called a 'run' on the bank, which may force it to call in loans in order to keep depositors happy.

Northern Rock became one of the first major victims of the 2008 financial crisis when customers began to demand their deposits back. Eventually the building society turned bank could no longer rely on the confidence of its depositors and the government had to launch a rescue attempt. In effect, the Chancellor of the Exchequer, Alistair Darling, nationalised the bank – taking it into public ownership – so that the government could provide the guarantees of safety and security that depositors needed. It emerged that part of the lack of confidence in Northern Rock was due to its balance sheet not being as transparent and accurate as everyone had thought. Northern Rock had lent money, in mortgages, to people who were at high risk of defaulting. These mortgages were liabilities and should have appeared on the balance sheet. Had they done so, they would have shown how much risk was being carried by the bank. However, Northern Rock kept some of its riskiest liabilities – those most likely to default – in a special way that meant it could keep them out of the public eye.

Many of these liabilities were kept 'off balance sheet' by being turned into what were called 'special investment vehicles'. Northern Rock kept these liabilities in a separate business called 'Granite' and registered in the offshore tax haven of Jersey. Although this was perfectly acceptable under accounting rules at the time, many people have seen it as a way of not declaring the true state of assets and liabilities that a balance sheet should show. The Prime Minister, Gordon Brown, promised that banks would have to show all of their liabilities in the future. In an interview with Sky News, he said that it was 'not acceptable' that banks could hide information in this way.

 All public limited companies have to produce a balance sheet and make it available to the public. Often these are available online. Go to the corporate website of a company in which you are interested and look at its balance sheet. See what judgements you can make about the business from the balance sheet. What else do you need to know to support your judgements?

Balance sheet

The **balance sheet** shows what the business has in the way of possessions and how these have been financed. It therefore shows the business how much it *owns* as against how much it *owes*.

Assets

The balance sheet may be divided into three parts – **assets, liabilities** and how **capital** has been raised. The first part measures the assets of the business – all the things that the business owns. They are either fixed – things like buildings and machinery used in production – or current – items like stocks of finished product or money owed that could be easily turned into cash. Some assets might be difficult to put a figure on. For example, when a business is sold, a value is often put on its 'goodwill'. This means the reputation of the business and its standing with customers. Assets include everything that a business owns to which a value can be attached, so in some cases items like goodwill will be included. Such assets cannot be physically touched so are called **'intangible' assets**.

In most cases an 'asset' entry also means a 'liability' entry in order to keep the balance. Clearly if a business buys £10,000 worth of stock, this increases its assets. At the same time, however, it has either paid for the stock out of cash reserves or, in most cases, still owes the supplier for the stock. This means that a £10,000 liability would appear as a **creditor**, making sure

Machinery is included in assets

that the stock (asset) and its cost (creditor) both appear.

Liabilities

The second part of the balance sheet shows liabilities – these are all the things that a business owes. These are either current – debts that must be paid back within a year, such as bank overdrafts or creditors – or long-term – debts that the business has more than a year to repay, such as long-term loans and mortgages. These are separated out in the account.

Working capital is calculated as current assets minus current liabilities. This figure is important as it shows the ability of the business to repay its short-term debts. If there is a positive working capital balance, then the business can meet its day-to-day needs. Suppliers, banks and other creditors will be confident that they will not only be paid but be paid on time. If working capital is negative, the business will struggle to pay its bills.

Net assets employed shows fixed assets (in this case £200,000) plus working capital (£40,000). From this figure the business then takes away its long-term liabilities to show its **net assets**. This is what the business is worth at this moment in time.

These assets have been financed in various ways, including loans, retained profit and share issues (see page 61). This is shown on the final part of the balance sheet, the capital account.

A balance sheet is a snapshot

Using the balance sheet

The balance sheet is of limited use because it can only ever be drawn up to represent the situation at a particular moment in time. It is not therefore looking at flows of finance or changes in such flows. To see what particular trends are, you would need to compare one balance sheet – at one point in time – with another one taken earlier or later. It is therefore often referred to as a 'snapshot', a picture taken at a point in time. Various stakeholder groups will have an interest in using the balance sheet. For example, it is important to:

- investors – to see how well their investment is performing and whether the business looks stable;

- creditors – to see how likely they are to have their debt repaid on time;

- managers – to help measure profitability, the cash situation, and to make comparisons with previous periods and other businesses; also to help them make key decisions;

- competitors – to compare their own performance against that of their rivals.

Summary

- The balance sheet is another important account for a business
- It shows what the business owns (assets) against what it owes (liabilities)
- It also shows how the capital invested in the business has been raised
- The balance sheet is only ever a 'snapshot' – a picture at a single point in time – so is of limited use
- Various stakeholder groups will find the balance sheet useful, but of much more use when combined with other financial information provided by the business

The capital account

BALANCE SHEET		
		TOTALS
Fixed assets	£	£
Land and buildings	100,000	
Machinery	70,000	
Vehicles	10,000	
Computers	10,000	
Intangible assets (goodwill)	10,000	
		200,000
Current assets	£	£
Debtors	10,000	
Stock	100,000	
Cash	10,000	
		120,000
Current liabilities	£	£
Creditors	60,000	
Overdraft	20,000	
		80,000
Net current assets (working capital)	£	£
Current assets minus current liabilities		40,000
Net assets employed	£	£
Fixed assets plus net current assets		240,000
Long-term liabilities		
Mortgages	40,000	
Long-term loans	10,000	
		50,000
Net assets		190,000
Capital account (shows these assets financed by...)	£	£
Share capital	120,000	
Retained profit	70,000	
Capital employed		190,000

Core knowledge

The balance sheet for a small business will be simple, that for a larger business more complex, but the principles are the same. The law requires limited companies to publish balance sheets with certain details, for example, the amount of finance raised through shareholders (shareholders' funds). Businesses that are not limited companies are not required to publish balance sheets and can keep their affairs private. However, a balance sheet might also be useful to them. The point of the balance sheet, in all cases, is to see what the business is truly worth.

There are three parts to a balance sheet (although often, because of the way in which it is laid out, it might look like more). Each part is linked to the others. They always show what the business owns (assets), what the business owes (liabilities) and how this has been financed. The most common way to set out a balance sheet is called the 'vertical balance sheet'. This shows assets, liabilities and capital in a vertical format so that it is clear where totals came from.

Balance sheets are important in helping investors (and others) to see how a company is developing. To do this, they need more than one balance sheet in order to make comparisons. They can see, for example, if a business is increasing investment, if it has enough to pay current debts or looks overstretched, if it has money to pay dividends or for future investment. The balance sheet also provides information for the managers of the company. They can see the value of capital and how it has been put to work in the business. They can see whether more finance needs to be raised or if debt needs managing better. They can also take into account other possibilities. If it looks, for example, like interest rates will rise or property prices fall, then they can look to adjust debt or mortgages accordingly.

And more

The type of business under consideration will have an effect on the balance sheet and investors need to take this into account when making judgements about a company. Just because a business has millions of pounds worth of assets does not necessarily mean that it is doing well. If it also has millions of pounds worth of debt – and if this debt is due shortly – the company could actually be in a lot of trouble. Companies are also affected by external events over which they have no control. A change in demand, or the introduction of new technology, could reduce the value of assets. Even intangible assets can be affected. If a customer found a foreign body in a chocolate bar, for instance, this could easily cause damage to the chocolate producer's reputation. Sometimes such damage to reputation can be as important as changes in the value of real, tangible assets.

You should always view published company accounts with caution – often they are not meant to reveal the real financial position of the business (internal figures will do this for managers). Window dressing is the practice of presenting accounts in as flattering a light as possible. Sometimes this just tidies up the accounts to make them easier to understand. At other times it hides the true position of the finances. For example, invoices may be issued early so that sales look like they are in the current year when in fact they should be included in the following period. Or extra cash can be injected into the company just before the end of the accounting period in order to make it look a better bet to investors. None of this is illegal unless it strays into actually falsifying accounts, in which case it is fraud.

Have a go!

Group activity

Each person in your group should choose a particular large company which has a website. Look through the website (in particular its marketing pages) and list the tangible and intangible assets of the business. Draw up a master list of possible tangible and intangible assets.

Discussion

Each person in your group should take the role of one stakeholder group and say why the balance sheet of a company might be of particular importance to that group.

Web-based activity

Using the corporate part of the website chosen for the group activity, find the latest balance sheet. Simplify the balance sheet so that a younger pupil could understand it.

Quickfire questions

1 What is meant by an 'asset'?
2 Explain the difference between fixed assets and current assets.
3 A strong brand name would be considered to be what sort of asset?
4 Define 'creditor'.
5 What is meant by a 'liability'?
6 Explain the difference between current liabilities and long-term liabilities.
7 Define 'debtor'.
8 What is meant by 'capital'?
9 Explain what is meant by 'working capital'.
10 Outline what is shown on the capital account.

Hit the spot

➤ Give one reason why the balance sheet may be of limited use.

➤➤ Explain why the balance sheet must always balance.

➤➤➤ Which do you think is most important to a business, tangible or intangible assets? Explain your reasoning.

Cracking the code

Assets These are all the things that the business owns.

Balance sheet. This shows what the business owns as against how much it owes.

Capital The amount of investment in the business.

Creditors People or organisations to which the business owes money.

Debtors People or organisations that owe money to the business.

Intangible assets Assets that cannot be physically touched, like a strong brand name or good reputation.

Liabilities These are all the things that the business owes.

Working capital This is current assets minus current liabilities and shows the ability of the business to repay its short-term debts.

Chapter 15
Ratios

IN THE NEWS

How does a business manage to lower the price of a product and yet increase its profit ratios? It is all down to keeping costs under control. Apple hit the market with a new product, the iPhone, that was different, fashionable and an immediate 'must-buy'. But it had its drawbacks – not least its lack of 3G capacity – and many criticised it for not doing as much as other phones in this area. It was also tied to a single provider in both the US and the UK. Nevertheless, the hype with which any new Apple product is launched meant that people were prepared to queue up just to own one.

But was it profitable? And is the new 3G phone, launched as a replacement, as profitable? Surprisingly, the 3G version, despite its more modern technology and greater flexibility, has a higher profit margin than the original, 2G phone. iSuppli, a market analyst, says that the manufacturing and component cost of the new phone has been reduced. By taking apart a 3G device and adding together the cost of its components, along with the costs of marketing the device, iSuppli has estimated that Apple has a 55% profit margin. It has estimated the cost of the iPhone (in the US) at $174.33, much lower than the estimated $227 cost of the original iPhone. These totals include materials and manufacturing costs, but do not include research and development, packaging and distribution. The real profit margin, when these are added in, along with the cost of the deal with the phone companies, brings the cost of the 8 gigabyte iPhone to approximately $225. As the price tag of an 8 GB iPhone in the US is $500, this represents a 55%

gross profit margin. Count in research and development and marketing (typically a further 7–9% on the cost) and this falls slightly, but is still impressive.

Some business commentators think that they can now see why Apple launched an 'inferior' version first. Its success meant that it covered most of the development costs and that marketing costs for the new version could also be reduced. As a result, the price of the new iPhone is lower than the original, but profit margins are considerably higher.

@ Do a web search for the price of the iPhone in different countries. Use a currency converter (like **www.XE.com**) to put all prices into pounds so that you can compare. Does the iPhone cost the same in every territory? Explain why you think this situation is so.

Profitability

When a business is looking at its profitability, it wants to know how much profit it is making on each sale. To do this it can look at its **profit margins**. (The margin is the amount of profit the business is making, expressed as a percentage; it is also called a ratio.)

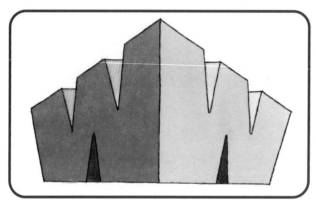

Which ratios are important to Walter's Widgets?

At Walter's Widgets Ltd, Wally is likely to be interested in two ratios – gross profit to sales revenue and net profit to sales revenue. Gross profit to sales revenue calculates the amount of profit the business is making once the cost of sales figure has been subtracted. This can also be called the **gross profit margin**. Net profit to sales revenue calculates the amount of profit the business is making once all costs have been subtracted. This can also be called the **net profit margin**.

Gross profit margin

These figures are taken from the profit and loss account. Below is the trading account for last year for Walter's Widgets Ltd.

Sales revenue	Wally's Widgets Ltd	£825,000
Minus Cost of sales	Opening stock 325,000 plus purchases 200,000 minus closing stock 100,000	£425,000
Gross profit		£400,000

The gross profit margin or gross profit to sales revenue ratio is worked out using the formula:

$$\frac{\text{Gross profit}}{\text{Sales revenue}} \times 100 = \%$$

so in this case is:

$$\frac{400,000}{825,000} \times 100 = 48\%$$

This figure tells Wally that his business is making 48p on each £1 of sales and that 52p goes on the cost of sales. Wally can then look at this year's trading account. He can see that sales revenue is up, but so is the cost of sales and so is his gross profit. To find out if he is more or less profitable, he must compare the percentages.

Sales revenue	Wally's Widgets Ltd	£925,000
Minus Cost of sales	Opening stock 100,000 plus purchases 450,000 minus closing stock 50,000	£500,000
Gross profit		£425,000

$$\frac{425,000}{925,000} \times 100 = 46\%$$

Wally knows that his business is actually now slightly less profitable, so can see that he needs to cut costs if possible.

Net profit margin

The net profit to sales revenue, or net profit margin, is worked out in a similar way. The formula for this is:

$$\frac{\text{Net profit}}{\text{Sales revenue}} \times 100 = \%$$

From the profit and loss account, the figures show:

Sales revenue	Wally's Widgets Ltd	£925,000
Gross profit		£425,000
Minus Expenses	Rent 75,000 Wages 100,000 Transport 25,000 Power 50,000 Fuel 50,000 Computers 35,000	£335,000
Net profit		£90,000

$$\frac{90,000}{925,000} \times 100 = 9.7\%$$

This means Walter's Widgets is making just 9.7p for each £1 sold. Whether this is good or not may depend on the product. Some products (like crisps) rely on high-volume sales with low margins. Other products (designer clothes, for instance) have few sales but high margins. Wally can also, as with the gross profit figure, compare this with both previous time periods and other businesses in the same industry.

Current ratios

Businesses (and their stakeholders) also want to know whether the business can pay its debts. The **current ratio** shows whether the business can meet its liabilities (debts) easily by turning assets into cash. These figures are taken from the balance sheet. This extract is from the balance sheet you looked at on page 77.

Current assets	£	£
Debtors	10,000	
Stock	100,000	
Cash	10,000	
		120,000
Current liabilities	£	£
Creditors	60,000	
Overdraft	20,000	
		20,000

The formula for working out the current ratio is:

$$\frac{\text{Current assets}}{\text{Current liabilities}}$$

This is usually expressed as a ratio rather than a percentage. It always helps if you can reduce one side to '1'. In this case it is:

$$\frac{120,000}{80,000} \text{ or } \frac{12}{8} \text{ or } \frac{3}{2} \text{ or } 1.5:1$$

This shows that Walter's Widgets can meet its short-term debts one and a half times over – a healthy position for a business. A ratio less than this would be a worry, more than this (say 3:1) probably means that too many assets are being held as cash.

Acid test ratios

The current ratio, as you can see, assumes that stock can be sold. This may not always be the case, particularly in the short run. The **acid test ratio** takes stocks out of the calculation and is a much sterner measure of a business's ability to meet liabilities. The formula is:

$$\frac{\text{Current assets} - \text{stocks}}{\text{Current liabilities}}$$

In this case, this would be:

$$\frac{120,000 - 100,000}{80,000} \text{ or } \frac{20,000}{80,000} \text{ or } 0.25:1$$

This shows that the business could have trouble paying off its debts. A healthy acid test ratio is seen as 0.5:1 to 1:1.

Summary

- Profit margins show the amount a business is making on each sale
- These are also called profitability ratios, as they compare sales revenue totals with profits
- Profitability ratios can be found by using the published profit and loss account of a business
- Comparisons between profitability ratios are often clearer if percentages are used
- Current ratios show the ability of the business to pay its debts
- Current ratios can be found by using the published balance sheet of a business
- The acid test ratio does not assume stocks can be sold, so is a more accurate indicator of the ability of the business to pay its debts

What is the **ratio** of teachers to pupils in your school or college?

Did you know...

When you are using financial ratios, the examination board will always provide you with the formulae that you need, so you don't have to worry about getting figures the right way round. Just make sure that you have a calculator.

Core knowledge

Businesses need to use the accounts that they prepare in order to see how well they are doing. They need to be able to use figures from the accounts to judge whether they are performing well or badly. Comparisons may be made to other businesses, to the performance in previous years, or between different products within a business. In the case of the iPhone, for example, Apple can compare the impact of the new model on the business to that of the old model. Using the figures on profit and loss accounts and balance sheets, businesses can find the answers to vital questions such as:

- Are they profitable and if so, how profitable?
- Have they improved profit?
- Are their finances sound, i.e. are they capable of paying their debts, not borrowing too much, not holding too much money in cash?

This is information that is vital to the various stakeholders in a business. Owners and managers want to see efficiency and profitability; creditors such as suppliers and lenders want to know that the business can pay its debts; customers want to know that the business can continue to provide quality products. The answers to these questions often lie in the use of financial ratios.

A ratio is simply one thing measured in terms of another. If there are 16 boys in your class and 8 girls, then the ratio of boys to girls is 16 to 8 or 2 to 1. In other words (as is obvious), there are two boys to each girl. This can also be shown as a percentage.

$$\frac{\text{Number of boys}}{\text{Number of girls}} \times 100 = \frac{16}{8} = 200\% \text{ i.e. twice as many boys as girls.}$$

You can see that you have to be careful with ratios as this can also be expressed as the ratio of girls to boys. In this case:

$$\frac{\text{Number of girls}}{\text{Number of boys}} \times 100 = \frac{8}{16} = 50\% \text{ i.e. half as many girls as boys.}$$

The reason for using a percentage is clear when the business tries to make comparisons as figures are not often as clear-cut as 2 to 1. For example, is a ratio of 89:98 better than 90:99? A percentage calculation shows us that the answer is:

$$\frac{89}{98} \times 100 = 90.8\%$$

$$\frac{90}{99} \times 100 = 90.9\%$$

You will see in the example of Walter's Widgets that this is important for a business when both sides of the equation (e.g. sales revenue and profit) increase.

And more

Although these are the key ratios for profitability and liquidity (current and acid test ratios are called 'liquidity ratios'), there are other ratios that are equally important to a business. Perhaps the other most important ratio is ROCE or Return on Capital Employed. This measures how efficiently the business is using the capital invested in it, so is a key ratio for investors. The formula is:

$$\frac{\text{Net profit}}{\text{Total capital employed}} \times 100 = \%$$

Investors can then compare efficiency with previous years, other similar businesses and other investments. Clearly if this percentage fell below bank interest rates, then it would be a better bet for an investor to open a bank account than invest in the business!

It is also important to know how managers and owners can make use of ratios when judging in which direction to take a business. To choose the most appropriate action, owners and managers need to weigh up the advantages and disadvantages. For example, cutting costs might look like a good bet, but this might also lead to less efficiency or lower quality if inferior raw materials are used. It is not always easy to increase revenue – a price increase might lead to less of the product being bought, sales and offers could sell more products, but at reduced margins. Ratios and accounts can be used to help predict what might happen and thus to make the business more efficient or more profitable, or both.

Did you know...

Always compare like with like – it would be pointless comparing a power station with a corner shop!

Have a go!

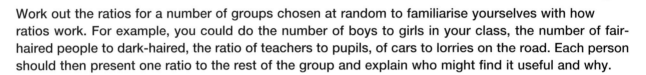

Group activity

Work out the ratios for a number of groups chosen at random to familiarise yourselves with how ratios work. For example, you could do the number of boys to girls in your class, the number of fair-haired people to dark-haired, the ratio of teachers to pupils, of cars to lorries on the road. Each person should then present one ratio to the rest of the group and explain who might find it useful and why.

Discussion

Which do you think is the most important ratio to a business, profitability or liquidity? Do you all agree? Is it the same for every business?

Web-based activity

Visit the corporate part of the website of a well-known company and, from its profit and loss account and balance sheet, work out its gross and net profit margins and its liquidity ratios. Would you recommend that someone invest in the company? Why?

Quickfire questions

1   Define what is meant by gross profit margin?
2   Define what is meant by net profit margin.
3   What is a ratio?
4   From which published account would you take the figures for profitability ratios?
5   How would you work out a profitability ratio?
6   Why do we use percentages to compare ratios?
7   What is a liquidity ratio?
8   From which published account would you take the figures for liquidity ratios?
9   How would you work out an acid test ratio?
10 Why is the acid test ratio important?

Hit the spot

➤   Describe how a business would work out its profit margins and give an example.

➤➤ Explain why a business would need to know its liquidity ratios.

➤➤➤ Identify three other groups which may need to know about the ratios of a business. Which of these do you think is the most important and why?

Cracking the code

Acid test ratio This compares assets (not including stock) and liabilities to show if the business can meet its debts. The formula is: current assets – stock/current liabilities.

Current ratio This compares assets and liabilities to show if the business can meet its debts. The formula is: current assets/current liabilities.

Gross profit margin This calculates the amount of profit the business is making once the cost of sales figure has been subtracted from total sales revenue.

Net profit margin This calculates the amount of profit the business is making once all costs have been subtracted.

Profit margins The amount of profit the business is making on sales, expressed as a percentage.

ADVANCED PEOPLE IN BUSINESSES

Chapter 16
Introduction to advanced people in businesses

In this section

Introduction to advanced people in businesses
Organising a growing business
Recruiting staff
Appraisal and training
Motivation

In this section of chapters you will be studying how larger companies deal with the people they encounter in business. Clearly, the people who work for the business, its employees, are an important group. Many large companies go as far as to state publicly that they recognise the importance of employees in making their business successful. A search of the internet using 'valuing our employees', or similar phrases, will result in many examples of such businesses.

So, why does a business feel the need to let everyone know that it believes its employees are so crucial? It could be that it hopes that the message gets out and the public views the business in a positive light. This might persuade some consumers that the business is a decent organisation and worth their custom. Alternatively, it might encourage those looking for employment to consider working for that particular business. Or it could be it just wants the world to know that it genuinely is a caring organisation.

Motivation

Whatever the reason, a large business needs to ensure it recruits the best people to work for it, trains them properly so they can do their work competently and treats them well so they are motivated and loyal to the company. Without motivation, a business will never get the best from its workers. Without loyalty, employees will leave on a regular basis, making it hard for teams to develop, besides pushing up recruitment and training costs.

There is no single answer to the question 'How do you motivate employees?' Each person is different, with differing needs and personal circumstances. For some it will be the wage that is the driving force, for others it will be other factors. The owner of a small business is likely to know his or her employees sufficiently well to have a good idea what needs to be done to keep them working efficiently. Close personal relationships are less likely to operate between manager and employee in larger businesses. However, many large businesses are encouraging managers to get to know their employees better. The 'them and us' way of thinking, where managers and workers distrust each other, is slowly breaking down in favour of more co-operative working.

Communication

Providing good communication is a theme that cuts through many of the chapters in this section. A large business can seem impersonal to an individual employee. Unlike small businesses, where it is likely that all the employees know each other, communications can be an issue. There is a sense of pulling together in a small business that cannot always be reproduced in larger companies. Businesses do, nevertheless, try to ensure that employees are kept informed, or at least they feel that they are. Businesses will spend time, effort and money producing company magazines or newsletters, purely to make employees feel they know what is going on.

Training for the workplace

Training

Many students might view training as giving each employee the necessary skills to be able to do his or her job properly. Training is that, but more besides. Training is used by business to motivate employees. Broadening a person's skill levels can make that person feel appreciated, even if there is no immediate prospect of putting the new skills into practice. What it does instead is raise that employee's interest levels in the work he or she does, increasing that person's efficiency. While it might not be thought of as training, changing employees' attitudes is an aspect of training. If a business wants its employees to take more responsibility for the quality of the work that they produce, it will have to train them. This training would not just be in the techniques they would use to check their own work, but would also be in getting them to realise how important this new way of doing things is.

People other than employees

Of course, employees are not the only people within a business, there are many others, shareholders for example. These people effectively own the business and, for most, their main consideration is how profitable the business is. Shareholders get money in two ways: from their annual or twice-yearly dividend and when they sell their shares for more than they paid for them. Most shareholders take the view that as long as the company in which they own shares is performing as well as other similar businesses, they are happy. Company directors represent shareholders' interests within the business.

Suppliers are important to a business, particularly when they provide raw materials or components that cannot easily be obtained elsewhere. Forging good working relationships with suppliers is important if a business is to be assured of continued supplies. We will read in Chapter 23 how a Japanese company takes it upon itself to ensure that its suppliers receive support if they are having difficulties. The principle of thinking about the long-term success of a business is central to this company.

Without customers, a business would fail to sell any goods. This might sound a ridiculous statement to make, but it does illustrate the importance of a business providing goods or services that its customers want to buy, at a price that they are happy with. Clever marketing can influence consumers' preferences. Establishing a successful brand name can convince consumers to buy one product rather than a competitor's, even if the price paid is higher and the quality no different. No business would be advised, though, to assume that its customers will continue to be loyal and buy its goods indefinitely.

Chapter 17
Organising a growing business

IN THE NEWS

Southern Demolition Company Ltd

Southern Demolition Company Ltd is a private limited company with headquarters at Byfleet in Surrey. The business was started in 1953 by Sidney Hunt Senior and it has expanded considerably since those early years. Southern Demolition is involved, as its name suggests, in the dismantling of buildings and other structures. If developers are to improve or change the use of an industrial area, they might need the services of a company like Southern Demolition. Buildings may need to be demolished to make room for other, more modern constructions to be put up in their place.

Demolition is sometimes seen as the poor relative of the construction industry. Some people view it as destructive and not really requiring any skill beyond brute force. This is far from the case. Many old buildings, for instance, contain dangerous materials such as asbestos. Employees who are used to remove this hazardous waste must be fully trained to keep themselves and others safe. By law, workers who remove toxic materials must have followed recognised courses and be fully qualified to do so. Demolition sites are also very dangerous places, so proper training is required to avoid injuries.

As managing director, Sidney Hunt, the son of the founder, has chosen to create a clear organisational structure, which is represented in its organisation chart (see next page). This diagram shows the breakdown of the business into its different departments or functions. The chart is published on the company's website, so anyone who deals with the business knows who is in charge of each function and what the different functions are. A customer making enquiries about a contract would, for instance, know whom to contact within the organisation. The chart might also be useful for those who work at Southern Demolition. Employees can see how the different functions work together and how their contribution fits into the whole organisation.

The chart also conveys a hidden message about Southern Demolition. It says: we are organised and have well-qualified staff. So, it could also be seen as a form of marketing. Potential customers who go on to the website might be influenced by the organisation chart. They may be more willing to use Southern Demolition because the chart makes it appear professional and organised.

@ Take a look at the
Southern Demolition website at
www.southerndemolition.co.uk

Span of control

The number of people which a manager directly supervises is called the **span of control**. We can see on Southern Demolition's organisation chart that the managing director, Sidney Hunt, has a span of control of many people. We cannot tell exactly how many are under Mr Hunt's direct control, as we don't know how many supervisors and subcontractors there are. It is clear, however, that Mr Hunt appears to have control of much of the business. The two other directors do not seem to have any **subordinates**, or at least the chart would suggest this.

It is unlikely that a managing director would be able to supervise every single employee within a business, unless the organisation was very small. A manager will often delegate responsibility to a subordinate, who will take control of a particular area of the business. In the case of Southern Demolition, we can see that the office manager has delegated responsibility for the office administration staff. Delegated responsibility means that the manager has the authority of the managing director to supervise the employees in that section. Sometimes the power of delegation allows the supervisor to make important decisions without referring to his or her **line manager** for permission. In other cases, there might be a limit on how much authority the supervisor has. But whichever system is used, the overall responsibility for the business lies with the managing director.

What is the ideal number of people that a manager should supervise? This can depend upon several things.

- *Physical location*. If a business is spread over a wide area, possibly having several sites, it may

not be easy for one manager to supervise many people. This would also apply to a business whose employees worked from home, or whose work took them away from their managers, such as engineers who service people's central heating boilers.

- *Complexity of tasks*. A manager might also find it difficult to supervise several employees who were highly skilled. They would probably be involved in complex work and need more detailed support and attention.

- *Ease of communication*. Generally speaking, the easier it is to communicate with employees, the wider the span of control can be. A manager dealing with employees who do not speak English, for instance, would not be able to have a wide span of control.

Layers of management

An organisation chart also shows how many layers of management there are. In the Southern Demolition chart, there are three distinct layers: the managing director, the other managers,

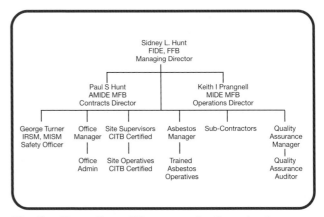

The Southern Demolition organisation chart

including the two directors, and finally the people on the bottom layer who work in the offices or at the building sites.

This three-layer system probably means that communications in this organisation are quite good. A decision made by the managing director could, in theory, be passed quickly on to everyone in the organisation. If a business has too many layers, communications can suffer and the organisation could become inefficient.

Summary

- Larger businesses often produce an organisation chart to show the different functions of a business
- Organisation charts make it easy for outside people to understand how the business is split up into different areas or functions
- The chart makes it easier for employees to know who is in charge of the different parts, or functions, of the business
- An organisation chart can also give the impression that a business is well organised and professional

Core knowledge

An organisation chart shows which subordinates are accountable to each of the line managers. The chart demonstrates how important each person is within the organisation. We call this a hierarchy and use terms like 'those at the top' and 'people at the bottom'. Usually those further up the hierarchy have more status and earn more than those lower down. With most hierarchies decisions tend to be made at the top and are communicated with those below. Some businesses do not like this structure as it does not encourage people lower down the chart to show initiative. Many layers of management can also mean it takes a long time for messages and ideas to travel to everyone in the business.

Some businesses have tried to reduce the number of layers within an organisation chart. This process is often called delayering. This can be achieved by looking carefully at which layers of management are not really required and removing them. Some managers may have assistants when there is no real need for this additional help. A manager might have insisted on having assistants to make him or her appear more important within the business. Delayering is a good opportunity to streamline the business as well as improve communications.

Some managers prefer to operate a flat hierarchy. This means removing some, or even all, of the layers of management. With this system, there is less distinction between managers and workers. Employees are allowed to take more responsibility for what they do and to show initiative. They are not supervised closely and are trusted to work well. Many employees prefer this method and respond positively to the trust the business has placed in them. Others workers can be reluctant to accept this new responsibility. They prefer to be told what to do by a line manager and not have to worry if anything goes wrong. Rather than thriving on problem solving in the workplace as others do, this type of employee would rather leave it to someone else to sort out. So, in order for a flat hierarchy to work successfully, it is important that employees have the right attitude towards working unsupervised.

Did you know...

The word hierarchy is Greek and was originally used to show who the important people in the Greek Church were.

And more

Matrix hierarchies. Some businesses have experimented with different kinds of management hierarchies. One such type is a matrix hierarchy. With this system, employees have more than one manager to check on them. If a group of employees is working on a project, they might have a specialist manager who monitors the skills they use and a project manager who checks on the progress of the assignment. For instance, a construction company might be building several hundred new houses on a site. The bricklayers might be responsible to a manager who knows how to deal with bricklaying issues as they arise. They might also be accountable to the project manager who will be concerned that the houses are finished on time and within budget.

Centralisation/decentralisation. As they develop and grow, many businesses realise that the decision-making power of the organisation has been centralised. This means that the key decisions on what the company does and what it plans to do in the future are made by a small group of people in one location. Quite often the people who are dealing with customers have a much better idea of what needs to be done to sell products for the best price. Some supermarket chains are starting to decentralise and allow individual store managers to make policy decisions. Rather than having to accept the 'official' price that the goods are sold for, managers can alter them if appropriate. If the weather is cold and rainy in an area, the manager of the local supermarket might decide to lower the prices of salads and barbecue food so they do not remain unsold.

Outsourcing. An increasing number of larger businesses are subcontracting work out to other organisations rather than doing the work themselves. This is known as outsourcing. A business may, for example, decide to pay a contractor to be responsible for cleaning its offices or use a human resource contractor to look after its recruitment. This allows the company to concentrate on its core business, the thing it is probably best at doing. In the example at the start of this chapter, we can see that the managing director of Southern Demolition is responsible for overseeing the work of the subcontractors that his business uses.

Inverted hierarchy. Some management experts argue that the organisation chart should be shown upside down, something called an inverted hierarchy. The idea of this is to get across the message that those lower down are, in fact, most likely to recognise when changes need to be made and how these changes should be implemented. These experts argue that the workers now at the top of the chart should be empowered to make their own decisions for the good of the business. While this is accepted in theory, many managers are reluctant to give up their status and power, so it is unusual to see an inverted hierarchy in practice.

Did you know...

Laurence Peter wrote a humorous book about business hierarchies. He suggested that employees keep on being promoted until they can no longer cope with the new level of responsibility they face and they remain in that job. The Peter Principle says that the posts in an organisation are held by managers who cannot really do their jobs properly!

Have a go!

Group activity

Working in groups, produce an organisation chart for your school that might be used within your school prospectus or information booklet to parents. Your chart should include everyone who works within the school, including support staff. When each group has finished, compare your charts. Do you have the same layers of hierarchy and spans of control? Discuss why groups might have different charts.

Discuss how you might rearrange the management hierarchy for your school. Give your ideas in a presentation to the rest of the class, or invite the head teacher or deputy to listen to your ideas.

Discussion

Discuss whether a flat hierarchy would work better than one with more layers in it.

Web-based activity

Search the web to find more examples of organisation charts. Comment on those you find in terms of the number of layers and the spans of control.

Quickfire questions

1   Describe the type of work that Southern Demolition undertakes.
2   Why is training important for Southern Demolition employees?
3   Describe two reasons why Southern Demolition's employees need to be well trained.
4   Explain, using Southern Demolition as an example, what is meant by a span of control.
5   What is decentralisation?
6   What is meant by delayering?
7   Give a reason why delayering might not work.
8   Give a reason why a business might outsource some of its jobs.
9   Give two reasons why a business might choose to decentralise.
10   Explain what a matrix hierarchy is.

Hit the spot

> Describe what is meant by an organisation chart.

> Explain how an organisation chart with several layers can result in poor communications.

> Discuss whether employees work better when they have less supervision.

Cracking the code

Span of control The number of people for which a manager is responsible.

Subordinates Those people who are below someone on an organisation chart.

Line manager The person to whom a subordinate is directly responsible.

Chapter 18
Recruiting staff

IN THE NEWS

Tesco

The supermarket chain, Tesco, employs over 300,000 staff in its stores, its distribution centres and head office in central London. The company sells food, clothing and household items. Tesco has recently started to offer other services, such as insurance.

Tesco believes that its employees should reflect the different cultures of the people who are its customers. The company is always trying out new ideas to attract employees from a wide range of backgrounds and religions. It is also keen to take on older workers who are past the traditional retirement age, and those who have disabilities. Tesco even has a panel of people who monitor the workforce to see how well the company is doing at achieving a mixed group of staff.

Tesco also tries to make sure everyone can work in a way that suits their circumstances. Employees are offered flexible working patterns, such as part-time roles. Job sharing and shift swapping are also

encouraged to make employees' **work–life balance** more acceptable. Tesco believes by providing flexibility employees will be loyal and remain with the company.

The method that Tesco uses to recruit and select new employees will depend upon the type of job vacancy. The business uses the internet as the main way to advertise for staff. Application forms can be downloaded from the internet, where applicants can also discover more about the benefits of working for the company.

Customer assistants

These are the people who help customers in supermarkets or who are pickers at one of Tesco's distribution centres. Pickers gather together the goods in a warehouse that need to be sent to stock Tesco stores around the country. The company website will have details of any vacancies, but local stores might also advertise the job where it can be seen by customers. Applicants wanting to become customer assistants are encouraged to visit the store or centre and talk to the people there.

If Tesco believes that the applicant appears to be suitable, he or she will be invited to an interview. The interview will be friendly and low pressured. Tesco managers will ask the applicant many questions. They will want to find out the applicant's background and work experience. The interviewers will also be interested to discover whether the person applying has the right attitude and skills to deal with people. The applicant will be able to ask questions about the job, working conditions and about Tesco too.

Managers

Applicants for managers' and head office workers' jobs are also advertised on the internet. Applicants for these posts are more likely to be drawn from a wider geographical area than those who are applying for assistant jobs. Unlike applications for assistant jobs, those applying for managers' jobs must do so online. Interviews for managers take place in central London. Tesco will pay the applicant's travelling expenses. As part of the process, applicants will be asked to complete a questionnaire on their attitudes to certain situations. Tesco uses this questionnaire to find out whether the person has the right approach to dealing with people and the other skills that they will need to do the job properly.

 Take a look at the Tesco careers website at **www.tesco-careers.com**

Did you know...

Chief Executive Sir Terry Leahy joined Tesco as a trainee manager in 1979 and rose through the ranks to the company's top position.

A large business like Tesco will have many vacancies to fill each year. Staff will leave for a variety of reasons and their posts will probably have to be filled. Recruiting applicants, and then selecting the most suitable of them, can be both time consuming and expensive. When a manager is showing somebody around the store, reading applications or interviewing, his or her time could be spent doing other things. Training a new employee is also expensive. The person will not work effectively until he or she has been trained. Training will often involve another employee showing the newcomer what to do, which means that person is also not working effectively.

Businesses want to attract the best staff, but they also want their employees to remain with them. The rate at which employees leave a business is known as **labour turnover**. A high turnover means a large number of employees are leaving each year. Large businesses like to see some turnover of staff. Having new people come with fresh ideas and enthusiasm can be good for a company, but large numbers of employees leaving is usually a sign that people are not motivated.

When somebody resigns, the business needs to decide whether that person should be replaced. It is possible that circumstances have changed

Did you know...

The name Tesco was made up from the initials of T E Stockwell, a tea supplier, and the first two letters of founder Jack Cohen's surname.

since the person leaving was recruited and the job is no longer needed. Technological advances might mean that much of the work the person did might be able to be done more efficiently using computer technology. If the managers do decide to replace the employee, they will want to get the best recruit for the job. They do not necessarily want an exact clone of the person who has left. It is an ideal time to stand back and think carefully about how the job has changed and where they want to see the business going in the future.

Large businesses are likely to produce two documents before they even think about advertising for a vacancy: a job description and a person specification. To save time, Tesco will probably have standard documents for jobs for which it recruits regularly, such as customer assistants. These documents will usually be sent out with the application form, or published online.

- *Job description.* This outlines the duties and responsibilities of a job. It will contain such information as the job title, the wage or salary, the day-to-day tasks, who the person's manager will be and whether the successful applicant will be supervising anybody else.

- *Person specification.* This document lists what skills, qualifications and experience are required for the job. It will often state whether each of these things is essential or desirable. Tesco managers might think it is essential that customer assistants have good communi-cation skills, but experience of shop working might be just as desirable.

Advertising

Once these documents have been produced, the business will need to let potential applicants know about the vacancy. Tesco relies on the internet to advertise any vacancies it has. Other businesses prefer to place advertisements in the media. The medium through which a job is advertised will usually depend upon the nature of the post being filled. If the job is low skilled and there are many people who could do the work, the advertisement will probably appear locally. This could be in a local newspaper or on a company notice board, inviting staff to pass on the details to anyone looking for work. If a more specialist job needs to be filled, it might be more appropriate to advertise more widely. Many industries have specialist newspapers or journals that employers might use to place their advertisement.

ASSISTANT CHEF, ANGLIA HOTEL

Cambridge   Full-time   Competitive salary

In this role you will assist the kitchen staff with the day-to-day running of the kitchen, and prepare food to a high standard. At the Anglia Hotel Restaurant, we offer an à la carte menu with daily specials to showcase the best local, organic food.

We are looking for someone who is passionate about food and about hospitality. Previous experience is not essential, but commitment and enthusiasm are.

We offer an excellent package of benefits, and you will receive a share of the service charge earned. We also run a training and development programme and encourage all staff to work towards further qualifications. The Anglia Hotel offers many opportunities for a rewarding career.

Did you know...

Four out of five Tesco employees shopped at the supermarket chain before getting a job there.

Summary

- The internet is becoming an increasingly important way for large businesses to attract job applicants
- Recruiting staff is expensive, in terms of both money and managers' time
- Businesses use application forms, interviews and different tests to help them determine the best person to fill a vacancy
- The way an employee is recruited will often depend upon the type of vacancy being filled

Core knowledge

Many businesses choose to recruit managers and supervisors internally. This means rather than advertise the job outside the organisation, they offer the post to someone who already works for the business. The attraction of recruiting managers this way is the company knows the applicant and his or her strengths. It avoids the situation of being taken in by someone who performs well at interview but then fails to live up to expectations when appointed to the job. There are ways of avoiding this situation, however, and these can be found in the section 'And more', below.

There are benefits of bringing in somebody new to the business rather than recruiting internally. Fresh ideas and new ways of doing things can be introduced into the organisation. Also, if someone was promoted internally, the person might not find it easy to command the respect of the co-workers with whom he or she has worked before.

Businesses rely on application forms to determine which of the applicants would be suitable to interview. This is known as the short list. The form will contain questions asking for details of the topics that the employer sees as being important. By doing this applicants must provide essential information, which they might not if they applied by writing a letter.

It is usual to ask for personal details from the applicants, such as their name, address and contact telephone numbers. Some items of information are considered too sensitive to ask as the business does not want to be accused of discrimination. For this reason, it is unlikely that age or date of birth will be requested, or whether the person is married. Sometimes businesses include a separate form asking for details of ethnicity, race and disabilities, so they can monitor if they are recruiting a good mix of people. This second form is kept apart from the main form and does not influence who is taken on.

Interviews vary according to the nature of the job to be filled. For a low-paid job, it may be little more than a short conversation with a manager. The applicant might be asked about his or her work experience and why he or she wants to work for the organisation. More skilled jobs might require a full day, or even two days, of tests and group interviews. The applicants will be placed in difficult situations to see how they perform. They might have to perform role-play exercises and other professional tests to see how competent they are. Sometimes the employer just wants to see how people respond under pressure.

Did you know...

It might be helpful to go back to Chapter 21 in Setting up a Business to remind yourself about how small businesses recruit staff.

And more

Psychometric tests. Some businesses are starting to use psychometric tests to find out more about the people who apply for jobs. Applicants are usually given a questionnaire to complete as part of the selection process. The answers the applicant gives to these questions can allow the employer to discover a great deal about those applying for the job. The test could determine what motivates the applicants, how they react to authority, how creative and imaginative they are and how open they are to learning new skills. Critics of psychometric testing say that those being tested can often work out which of the answers the employer is looking for and not answer the questions honestly.

Probationary period. When an applicant is appointed to a job, the business might decide to take them on for a probationary period. This means the employee's contract is not made permanent until the applicant has proved that he or she is capable of doing the job properly. If the business finds that the person is not shaping up, the managers are able to terminate the contract at the end of the probationary period. This is really an insurance policy for the business; it will not be left with someone whose application form, references and interview are all good but who fails to live up to expectations when appointed, Probationary periods are usually used only for senior jobs within a business. The problem with probationary periods is that they can discourage people from applying for the job. Accepting the job and working a probationary period does have a risk. The successful applicant would have to resign from his or her current job and if they failed the probationary period they would end up jobless.

Recruitment agencies. These are businesses that specialise in finding employees, which saves managers the task of having to do it themselves. In return for recruiting a suitable person, the agency will receive a fee from the employer. This, in a way, is a form of outsourcing which was covered earlier in the book. By using a recruitment agency, a business can concentrate on more important jobs, while the agency spends time searching through application forms and interviewing potential candidates. A recruitment agency can save a business time and effort.

Have a go!

Group activities

Produce a suitable application form to use to recruit teachers to your school.

Imagine Tesco has asked you to come up with a way of finding out how well applicants for customer assistants' posts are able to deal with people. In a group, come up with as many tests and activities that you think would be suitable. Choose the best two and produce all the paperwork you would need to run both of them.

Produce a person specification for a Tesco customer assistant. Show which of the items should be essential and which desirable.

Discussion

Discuss how useful formal interviews are in determining who is the best person for the job. Are there better ways that could be used?

Web-based activity

Compare the recruitment process used by Tesco with the other major supermarkets. Produce a list of similarities and differences.

Quickfire questions

1 Where is Tesco's head office?
2 How does Tesco advertise for its staff?
3 What job does a Tesco picker do?
4 What is a job description?
5 What is a probationary period?
6 What does a recruitment agency do?
7 Give two items of information that might be asked for on an application form.
8 Explain why a firm might be worried about a high labour turnover.
9 Explain why an applicant's date of birth is not usually included on an application form.
10 Give two disadvantages of recruiting managers internally.

Hit the spot

> What is meant by labour turnover?

> Explain two ways a business might reduce the amount of labour turnover.

> Discuss whether advertising vacancies on the internet is the best way of attracting applicants for a job.

Cracking the code

Work–life balance Ensuring a reasonable split between the time a person spends working and other family and leisure activities.

Labour turnover The rate at which employees leave a business. If a business had 80 employees and 20 left during the course of a year, the turnover would be 20/80, or 25%.

Chapter 19

Appraisal and training

IN THE NEWS

British Gas Services

British Gas Services (BGS) is part of British Gas, which is owned by the Centrica Group of Companies. British Gas supplies gas and electricity to households and businesses around the UK and Europe. It is the UK's largest supplier of fuel. BGS is not directly involved in supplying gas, but is responsible for installing and maintaining gas appliances, such as boilers and cookers.

BGS needs to have the right staff in order to deliver these services effectively. Because of the hazardous nature of gas and electricity, BGS employees need to be fully trained and motivated. As the BGS employees deal directly with British Gas's customers, it is important that they create the right impression. If customers feel that the service they receive from BGS staff is poor, this could have a serious impact on British Gas. Consumers are always looking for the best deal from their fuel suppliers and will switch to another if they are unhappy with the service they are receiving. So it is important that BGS employees not only have good technical knowledge but also good people skills. It is for this reason that the British Gas Academy was created, where BGS employees are trained.

The British Gas Academy trains both new recruits and established employees who need to be updated.

New recruits are taught the relevant skills they will need to do their jobs and learn about British Gas and the gas industry. The training also covers communication and problem-solving skills. Trainees are taught how to listen to people and to deal with them politely. BGS also has an apprentice system, where recruits work alongside an experienced employee to learn 'on the job'. All employees regularly attend refresher courses or training to update their skills. The need for these courses is identified at the regular review meetings that each employee holds with his or her manager.

 Take a look at the British Gas Academy website at
www.britishgasacademy.co.uk

BGS recognises that it costs more to recruit and train a new employee than it costs to retain an established one. So it makes financial sense not only to attract the best people as employees but also to ensure they are happy and satisfied in their work so that they are not tempted to go elsewhere. Providing employees with good quality training so they can do their work confidently is a good way of both making staff happy and keeping the company in business. This is especially true in a **competitive market** like gas services.

BGS has an established training programme for new recruits to the industry. They need to be taught the basics of their jobs at the training academy. Dealing with existing employees is another matter though. BGS needs to check on established employees to make sure that they are fully trained to be able to undertake everything that is expected of them. This is usually done at the employee's performance review, or appraisal, meeting.

Performance management

Managers use performance management meetings to try to get the best out of each employee. The employee might be asked a series of questions about his or her work since the last review. The manager is trying to find out if there are any gaps in the employee's skills that need to be addressed. Evidence could be looked at where the employee's performance falls short of the required standard. In the case of BGS, this might be an engineer who has not been as friendly to a customer as the company would have liked. Or a job that the engineer undertook needed to be redone because it was below standard. When this is the case, training needs will be identified. This is particularly true in an industry, such as gas servicing, where technology is changing all the time and skills need to be updated.

It is normal at these performance review meetings for objectives or targets to be agreed between the reviewer and the person being reviewed. These targets give a focus to the employee and should be achieved before the next meeting. The target might be to undertake some form of training, or possibly to increase the speed at which jobs are completed. Some businesses use the performance management meetings to decide whether an employee's wages should increase. If targets are achieved or exceeded, the employee is paid more. The increase may be permanent or in the form of a one-off bonus.

Summary

- Employees need to be trained not just in the work they do but also in how to deal with customers
- It is not just new employees who need to be trained; all workers need to have their skills updated on a regular basis
- Performance management meetings allow a business to check on how well the employee is doing his or her work and what additional training is needed
- Objectives are often set for the employee to reach before the next performance management meeting. Wage increases might depend upon reaching these objectives

Core knowledge

When a business trains an employee, it must decide upon the best way to do this. Traditionally, training was undertaken using the apprentice system. This involved a recruit working alongside an experienced worker, who would pass on their skills. This approach is known as on-the-job training. It was recognised, however, that apprentices might not be getting the best form of training. Older employees might not be fully up to date with modern techniques and they would sometimes pass on bad habits to the apprentice. For these reasons, many apprentice schemes included the trainee working at college, sometimes called day release, to learn modern practices.

Training while working is known as on-the-job training, while training in a classroom or similar place is called off-the-job training. In the case study, BGS uses its own training facilities to train not only new recruits but established staff. Because the workers are not actually undertaking real work, they are receiving off-the-job training. BGS probably finds it can ensure that the quality of training is better at the British Gas Academy than relying wholly on the apprentice system.

When a new recruit joins a business, he or she will probably be given induction training. This is the training a person first receives to make sure they are as informed about the business as established employees. The new recruits might be shown a video about what the company does, so that they are familiar with the things that are important. Health and safety issues will be explained. Recruits will be given safety information, such as what they should do if the fire alarm sounds. The company might also use this training to explain company rules on phoning in sick or what to do if employees need to take time off work for family or other reasons.

Businesses want their employees to be efficient, which means they want them to be able to undertake their work quickly and accurately. If an employee is not skilled enough to do the work, or

The apprentice system

lacks motivation, this can have a negative impact on the business. Employees are more likely to make mistakes that result in wastage of materials and time spent re-doing the work. It is also more difficult to introduce changes to the business when employees do not feel that they are properly qualified. Spending money training and motivating employees can mean that they will be less likely to resist change and will support the company.

Performance management, or appraisal as it is sometimes called, is frequently used by managers to try to get the best out of their employees. At appraisal meetings, the manager and employee have the opportunity to talk about what has gone well and not so well over the last year. The employee's training needs will be considered. It may be that the employee did not do well last year because he or she was not competent in some aspects of the job. The interview will probably come up with objectives that need to be achieved in order to improve. The manager may also set a target that the employee has to reach by the time of the next interview. A shop assistant in a computer store may be set the target of increasing the sales he makes by 10% or getting to know more about some of the products. This way he can be more helpful to customers.

And more

Types of performance management. How a business conducts its performance management meetings will vary between organisations. In one business a manager might simply have an annual meeting with each employee. This meeting could take the form of a brief conversation with one or two objectives, or targets, set at the end. The whole process might then be forgotten until the next meeting in a year's time. Other businesses will take the process a lot more seriously. The manager, or reviewer, will have a structured questionnaire to work from in the interview. The manager and employee will have to decide how well the last year's objectives were achieved. This would be particularly important if the employee's salary was linked to reaching these objectives, which is often called performance-related pay. When new objectives are set for the forthcoming year, a development plan will be created. This will outline what needs to be done so the objectives can be achieved, which will probably include some form of training. It will also set out a time scale for achieving these things and a date when progress can be checked.

One difficulty that can arise with performance-related pay is that it is not always possible to determine just how much of a contribution an individual employee has made. Many employees work as a group or team and it is not easy sometimes to work out just who has done what to make the team successful. Reviewers have to be careful that an individual is not singled out for reward.

Workforce planning. A business that is forward looking cannot afford to be caught out by not having enough skilled employees when it needs them. For this reason, many larger businesses choose to undertake workforce planning. It can take several months to recruit a suitable person and to train him or her so that they are in a position to start work. So, if the company is expecting to see an increase in demand for its products or services, it is important that there are enough trained people when they are needed. If a business was planning a big promotional campaign to increase the sales of its product, the campaign would need to ensure that there were enough products available, which would probably mean enough staff to produce the goods.

Have a go!

Activity

Use a local business with which you are familiar. Alternatively, use a fictitious business. Set up a first-day induction training programme for somebody new to the business. Decide what the person needs to do and produce a day's programme with timings.

Discussion

Discuss which type of training is better: on-the-job or off-the-job.

Web-based activity

Research on the web how companies conduct their performance management, or appraisal. Produce an information sheet or booklet giving practical advice to businesses new to performance management.

Quickfire questions

1   Which company owns British Gas?
2   What type of work is undertaken by BGS?
3   Give two reasons why BGS employees receive training in how to deal with people.
4   What is the name of the centre where BGS employees are trained?
5   Why do experienced employees also have to receive training?
6   Give an example of off-the-job training.
7   How does the apprentice system of training work?
8   What is performance-related pay?
9   Explain how training can help motivate staff at BGS.
10 Give two reasons why businesses hold performance management meetings.

Hit the spot

> What is meant by on-the-job training?

> Explain two ways in which off-the-job training might be delivered.

> Discuss whether having a system of performance management helps motivate employees.

Cracking the code

Competitive market An industry where there are many companies, each trying to attract customers.

Chapter 20
Motivation

Egg Banking – the 10:10 approach

Egg Banking plc is the largest internet-only bank in the world, employing 2500 people in three UK locations. The bank makes its money by encouraging savers to deposit money in one of its internet accounts and then issuing loans to customers. Egg is owned by the pension and financial services giant Prudential, or The Pru as it is often called. Banking is a very competitive business, with customers becoming increasingly willing to deal with foreign banks to get the best deals.

About half of Egg's employees deal directly with customers. If customers have any queries about their accounts, they will phone or e-mail one of the contact centres to have their questions answered. Another quarter of the employees are involved in IT work within the business. It is very important for an internet bank that the computer systems are functioning properly and safely. Egg has to be sure that criminals do not attempt to withdraw funds from other people's accounts and that there are secure records of all transactions. The remaining staff members are finance specialists. Banks will need employees who deal with such matters as risk assessment, which means calculating if a borrower is likely to pay the money back. They will need marketing and human resource specialists and professional managers, who have a good knowledge of the financial services business.

Egg recognises that it can be successful in a competitive market only if its employees are prepared to deal effectively with its customers. Egg believes that the only way you get the best from your employees is to allow them to develop within the business. The management at Egg realises that if the employees are not motivated, the business will suffer. Poorly motivated employees are less likely to be **loyal** to the company. This would probably result in employees regularly leaving the business and having to be replaced.

10:10 is how Egg describes the way in which employees and the company all benefit from working together. Each employee, and Egg itself, aims to achieve 10 out of 10. By enabling its employees to become motivated so they can reach their personal goals, Egg reaps the rewards of increased profits. So how does Egg manage to motivate its employees?

The company tries to create a working environment for employees so that they can get satisfaction from the challenges of their work. The line managers are crucial in helping the employees reach their potential. The managers are expected to have a good relationship with employees so that they get to know them well. Managers must understand what makes each of their subordinates tick and what drives them. In schools, students learn in different ways – some like to watch how things are done, then copy it themselves, others prefer to read about it and learn that way. It is the same with adults: they have different learning preferences. Egg managers are expected to find out the best way to train and motivate each individual so that each can then focus on high performance at work.

Take a look at the Egg website at
www.egg.com

Did you know...

The first online banking service was set up in New York in 1981. The Nottingham Building Society offered the first UK internet banking facilities in 1983.

Egg believes that its business will be successful only if its employees are well motivated. This is why it calls its programme to motivate staff 10:10. If the employees enjoy their work and are committed to the business, they feel good about themselves and Egg benefits too. Both their employees and Egg get 10 out of 10.

This might sound like commonsense, but not all businesses operate this way. Some take the view that time and money spent on keeping employees happy and content cause a reduction in profits. If you provide good facilities for employees such as a restroom or staffroom, they will be more inclined to enjoy these than get to work. Similarly, training in team building is seen by some as just a waste of the business's money.

Motivation is about getting people to work effectively because they want to. To help motivate its people, Egg makes sure that employees operate in an environment where they are able to:

● plan for themselves;

● work well with managers;

● enjoy their work;

● be rewarded for their efforts;

● feel they have the power to create change.

Egg refers to this as 'unleashing the power of people'. This power of people is achieved through good leadership and empowering employees to make changes they feel would improve their own performance and that of Egg. This means being willing to trust employees to work in the business's interests. Employees are given work to do that interests them and which they do well. This way the employee is likely to do a better job and to be more efficient. But, of course, this relies on the manager knowing each employee well.

Did you know...

The Prudential Mutual Assurance Investment and Loan Association, now known as The Pru, was set up in 1848 in London to lend money to both professional and working people.

What is motivation?

Motivation is the skill, or some say the art, of getting people to do things because they want to, rather than having to be told to do them. Employees who are motivated can see the benefit to themselves of working at their highest level of performance. At its most basic level, motivation in the workplace is linked to pay, or **remuneration**. It is the attraction of the weekly or monthly wage that drives some employees. They enjoy the things their wages can bring, such as holidays and consumer goods. These people work well because they do not want to give up their lifestyles which would happen if they lost their jobs.

Much research has been carried out on what factors drive employees to become motivated. There is no clear single method by which a business might guarantee being able to motivate its staff. We're all different, after all. What is clear, though, is that wages might motivate some people, but most others are driven by other factors. For some people, the amount you get paid is far down on the list of priorities. People who work for charities or undertake voluntary work probably do not value their job in terms of how much income they receive for doing it, if they get paid at all. Certain jobs are renowned for not being well paid, but still they attract motivated, qualified professionals. Nursing is a good example of this. Clearly, there must be something about the work that compensates nurses for the shortfall in their salaries.

In the Egg case study, we see that the company recognises that the working environment is important. The environment would include not only suitable heating and lighting in the workplace but factors such as feeling valued by the management, which make people feel comfortable. These features are often called **hygiene factors**. It is argued that without hygiene factors being satisfied, you will not be able to motivate staff. Being paid on time at the agreed rate is another example of a hygiene factor. If you were unsure you would receive your pay cheque at the end of the week, would you give your boss your best?

A cold, unpleasant work environment does not motivate employees

Summary

- Employees work best when they are motivated
- Poorly motivated staff are more likely to leave a business, resulting in having to spend time and money recruiting and training new staff
- Some businesses believe that spending money on motivating employees increases costs and reduces profits

Core knowledge

The way employees feel about their job and their workplace determines how motivated they are. There is a clear link between job satisfaction and productivity. Job satisfaction depends partly on tangible rewards – for example, how much a person is paid and what benefits they receive. However, job satisfaction also depends on the culture of an organisation. This means the things that make the business distinctive and make the people who work there proud to do so. People can be motivated by many factors. These are just a few examples.

- *The style of management*. At Egg, managers are encouraged to get to know their subordinates well. Employees are consulted about changes and they play a role in making key decisions in the business. They are made to feel that their contributions are valued within the business. This approach to management is often called a **democratic** style. Not all managers, however, operate this way. Some believe that consulting employees is both time consuming and unnecessary. Such managers would probably argue that they are paid to manage, so this is what they should do. This **autocratic** management style usually involves issuing instructions and expecting employees to follow them without question. Most employees are better motivated by the democratic style – they are more likely to accept change if they feel that they have had a say in the process. Nevertheless, some employees prefer not to have the responsibility that decision making brings.

- *Training and development*. Most employees like to feel that they are developing in their work. They want to become more competent at doing what they do so they are more expert in their job. We saw in Chapter 49 that BGS believes that all employees need to be trained throughout their careers if they are to keep their skills up to date. Training an employee shows the person that the business values him or her, and can lead to improved motivation.

- *Good communications*. As businesses grow, communications can become a problem. This is particularly true when there are many layers in the organisation chart. It can take time for messages and ideas to trickle down the hierarchy until they reach those at the bottom. If employees feel that they are out of the loop they can get the impression they are undervalued and their motivation levels fall. Businesses can overcome this problem in many ways. Many large businesses issue newsletters or even newspapers, while notice boards can keep people up to date. An intranet is another option, or operating a system of managers to brief employees regularly about what is happening in the business.

- *Regular feedback and appraisals*. If performance management is undertaken properly, rather than being seen as a threat, it can actually motivate employees. The regular meetings are opportunities for the manager to recognise the importance of the employee's contribution. Everyone likes to be told that they are doing a good job and people will be motivated by this.

- *Opportunities for employees to socialise*. This can take the form of team working or even having places at work where people can meet during their breaks. Some businesses go as far as having social clubs, often with sporting or gym facilities, where employees can socialise.

A pleasant break room can increase job satisfaction

And more

Many businesses believe that teambuilding is a good way to motivate individuals. If you can get everyone in your business to feel part of a team, the theory is you will get more out of them. Teams build motivation in people for several reasons.

- There is a social aspect to working in a team. People often find it more rewarding to work with others than alone.

- Teams stimulate fresh thinking and ideas. Working with others will often throw up different ways of looking at problems and how they might be solved.

- People will feel loyalty to the team and not want to let others down. This helps improve things like absenteeism, as well as increasing motivation levels.

- Team working brings out the competitive element in individual members. If this is managed properly the competition can help drive performance.

- Working in a team brings a sense of belonging and makes people feel valued.

Working as a team can be valuable

Have a go!

Activity

Produce a list of ten ways in which a business can motivate its staff. Make this into a PowerPoint presentation.

Discussion

'Teambuilding exercises are just an opportunity for employees to have a good time and they offer no real advantages to businesses.' Discuss how true you feel this statement is.

Web-based activity

@

Many companies use newsletters or magazines to keep their employees informed about what is happening in the business. Look on the internet for examples of these communications. Produce a report on what can be found in these newsletters and magazines.

Quickfire questions

1 What type of bank is Egg?
2 What type of work takes place at Egg's contact centres?
3 What is meant by employee motivation?
4 What is meant by hygiene factors?
5 What is phishing?
6 How can regular appraisals raise an employee's motivation?
7 Give an example of how the style of management can motivate an employee.
8 Give two reasons why businesses want to keep employees from leaving.
9 Give two reasons why people can work better in a team than individually.
10 Explain how Egg's 10:10 system works.

Hit the spot

⊚

> Describe what is meant by employee motivation.

>> Explain two ways a business might motivate an employee.

>>> Discuss whether increasing the rate of pay is the best way to motivate employees.

Cracking the code

Loyal Being willing to remain with a business and support it.

Remuneration Another term for wages, salaries and other benefits employees receive.

Hygiene factors The things that make people comfortable in their work so they can get on with their jobs.

Democratic A management style where employees are consulted and asked for their views on the business.

Autocratic A style of management where employees are told what to do and are not involved in any decision making.

ADVANCED OPERATIONS MANAGEMENT

Chapter 21
Introduction to advanced operations management

In this section

Introduction to advanced operations management
Production methods
Efficiency and lean production
Benefits and challenges of growth
Maintaining quality assurance in growing businesses

We have already seen that the manufacturing industries in the UK are becoming less important. The amount of money earned by the service, or tertiary, industries, however, is increasing steadily. You might remember that this process is called deindustrialisation. Manufacturing still takes place and has a role to play in Britain, but it has experienced many changes since it was the key industrial sector.

In this section of chapters we will be looking at manufacturing businesses and discovering the changes that have taken place. Much of this change has to do with the way in which products are made. Technology has revolutionised manufacturing. Routine tasks can be performed by computer-controlled machinery or robots. This has resulted in employees becoming less important in the production process than they were a generation ago. There has also been a change in the relationship between managers and employees. These two groups of people are more likely to co-operate than would have been the case 20 years ago. Many of the ideas and ways of doing things have evolved from the way that Japanese manufacturers are organised. It should be noted, though, that the principles that are covered in this section can often apply equally well to service industries.

A common business objective is to achieve growth. This is often the case for one or more of these three reasons:

- to sell a larger number of goods and, thereby, make more profit;

- to gain a larger market share, so the business has some control over the market;

- to reduce the cost involved in making each item.

Small businesses, therefore, have an incentive to grow bigger, even if it is done purely to make the owner feel that he or she has been successful in creating such a large company. But the very act of growing brings with it the types of problem for a manufacturing business that it would not have encountered when it was small.

Standardisation

Standardisation is a theme that cuts across much of the material covered in the next few chapters. In a way it is the complete opposite of job production, which we studied in Unit 1, Setting up a Business. You may remember that job production involved making a single item to suit a customer. We used the example of builders re-fitting a kitchen. The units and tops would have to be adjusted to suit the shape of the room, as would the water and gas pipes and electricity sockets. With standardisation, the same-size components are used as much as possible to avoid having to make adjustments. A manufacturer of flat-pack furniture, for instance, would attempt to use the same parts in the wardrobes that it manufactures as it does for chests of drawers it sells. By reducing the number of types of components it uses, it can save money and simplify the production process. Standardisation can also be applied to labour, in other words, the employees. If jobs are kept the same as much as possible, the worker can become competent very quickly at doing that job. This saves on training and also allows employees to swap between jobs without it being a problem.

they are not really making a useful contribution and feel alienated from their work. It is not unknown for the quality of products to suffer when this form of production is used.

Mass production

Mass production

Producing very large amounts of a single product, or mass producing, allows manufacturers to make the goods cheaply and quickly. This is usually achieved by having each employee concentrating on a small part of the production process. The product then moves from one work station to the next until it is completed, often on a conveyor belt. This system of manufacturing has enabled the price of products to be reduced for the consumer. A car might still be an expensive item to buy, but if the old ways of making cars had been maintained, only the extremely rich would have been able to afford to buy a car these days.

Mass production is not without problems, however. Assembly lines, once set up, are notoriously difficult to change if the demand for the good falls and another product must be made. So the managers of the business must be confident that there is sufficient demand for the product before considering mass production. Working on a mass production assembly line can be very repetitive too. Workers are expected to perform a small task over and over, which can be extremely boring. Employees might believe that

Lean production methods

Lean production methods were introduced by Japanese manufacturers to overcome the problems they discovered when they studied American and UK businesses. Companies, such as Toyota, wanted to produce goods with the lowest possible costs, but recognised that if the company was not careful it could create a production process where the work was so dull and repetitive that employees would lack the motivation to work well.

Lean production is really about keeping costs as low as possible by continually looking for ways in which small cost savings could be made. No change is dismissed as being too small and insignificant. If a cost saving can be made then, it is argued, there must be waste, even if this waste is simply someone's time that could be better used.

It is not just the managers who are told to look for ways to save costs by reducing waste. It is felt that those who operate the machines and produce the goods are more likely to be aware of how improvements can be made. Indeed, employees who work for a lean production company are empowered to accept responsibility. This means they have far more authority than an employee in a conventional business. Empowering employees is also a way of making their work more interesting and increasing their loyalty to the business.

IN THE NEWS

Ben & Jerry's Ice Cream

Ben & Jerry's is an ice-cream manufacturer, based at the luxury end of the market. The business was started in 1978 by two friends, Ben Cohen and Jerry Greenfield, and it grew quickly. Within ten years of starting, the business had a turnover of nearly $50 million. The business is now owned by the **conglomerate** Unilever.

Ben & Jerry's ice cream has always been presented as a fun product. The business regularly develops new flavours and ditches those which have lost their appeal. The names given to the ice cream are jokey and reflect the fun image of the business. Names include Fossil Fuel, Cherry Garcia, Chunky Monkey and Phish Food. The ice cream is made in batches of about 5000 litres, enough for around 8000 pint cartons. The basic ice cream base is produced in large containers, or vats, using good-quality ingredients. The milk used in Ben & Jerry's ice cream comes from selected farms close to the factory. Later in the process, flavours, chunks and swirls are added to give the ice cream its distinctive look and taste. Ben & Jerry's ice cream uses large chunks of chocolate, cookie dough and similar ingredients to give the product an unusual texture when it is eaten. Members of the public are encouraged to experiment with the flavours when the company's factories have visitors' days.

The production processes

The processes the ingredients go through to become Ben & Jerry's ice cream are as follows:

1 Milk is collected from farms and stored in refrigerated 25,000 litre storage units.
2 Milk is blended with other ingredients, including sugar and egg yolks.
3 Mix is heated to remove any bacteria that might be present.
4 Blend is then homogenised to break up fat particles.
5 At this stage the flavours are added to the ice-cream mix.
6 Mix is then frozen and ice cream produced.
7 Chunks of chocolate, fudge and other ingredients are added to the ice cream.
8 If the ice cream has swirls, these are produced in the variegator.
9 Pint cartons are filled and lids fitted.
10 Ice-cream cartons are deep frozen to allow them to be transported.
11 Before they are dispatched, sample cartons are opened and tasted to check the quality is right. Pint cartons are bundled into eight packs and dispatched.

Take a look at the Ben & Jerry's website
at **www.benjerry.co.uk**

As a manufacturing business grows and needs to produce more, it will probably look at the methods it uses to make the goods. Most likely it would not make commercial sense simply to buy larger quantities of equipment and continue to make products the same way it did when it was a much smaller operation. One advantage of growing large is that businesses can achieve **economies of scale**. This means it can be cheaper to make each product when larger amounts are made. You will be able to find out more about economies of scale in Chapter 24.

Machinery and automation

A growing business will look for ways in which production can become more efficient. Ben & Jerry's makes ice cream differently now than it did when it started in 1978. One thing that has changed is the greater use of equipment and **automation**. Machinery is used whenever possible as it is quicker and therefore more economical than using more labour-intensive methods. It is also much easier to maintain quality using machinery. In the case of ice cream and other food manufacturing, using machinery extensively can avoid contamination of the product.

Quality

Ben & Jerry's has a reputation for producing top-quality ice cream and this reputation must be protected. Quality control is important to the company, but so is its reputation for being an ethical business. The ingredients that it uses have to be of good quality. It only uses milk from controlled herds of cows from local farms. The eggs it uses are free range and it uses fair-trade goods for some of its other ingredients.

Batch production

The advantage of making batches of ice cream is that a wide range of flavours can be made using the same equipment. There does not have to be a separate production run for each flavour. Also, as flavours become more or less popular, different quantities can be made to suit the demand for each type of ice cream.

- Ben & Jerry's ice cream is marketed as a fun product at the luxury end of the market
- Production methods for large businesses can be more efficient than those of smaller businesses
- Batch production allows machinery and equipment to produce a variety of products without having to have separate production runs for each product

Core knowledge

Ben & Jerry's produces ice cream in large batches. Not all mass producers make their products this way; some find it better to use flow production methods.

This is the method used by most car manufacturers, as well as companies that produce many household appliances, such as washing machines. While some minor changes can be made to the product as it is being made, **flow production** is more suited to items that are standardised. This means the products are identical.

The term flow gives a big clue to how this system operates. Products are made continuously along an assembly line, moving or flowing from one stage of production to the next. This is usually in the form of a conveyor belt carrying the partly made product from one worker to the next. If the product being made is heavy, an overhead monorail might be used instead for all or part of the journey around the factory.

So, in the case of a car, the chassis will start the process and as it moves around the factory, a different part will be added. Suspension, steering, brakes, wheels and hundreds of other parts will be assembled as each vehicle passes through different areas of the factory. Some of the components for the car might be assembled using flow production elsewhere and brought to this assembly line. This would include items such as engines and metal panels. Alternatively, parts might be brought in from other manufacturers rather than being made by the company.

The advantage of flow production is that **division of labour** can be used. When each worker concentrates on one particular job and becomes expert at doing it, we say this is an example of division of labour. Workers can be organised so that they are responsible for adding a single item on the product as it moves around the factory. An employee's job might be to fit the windscreen on the car. This person would have the necessary tools to hand and because the job is repeated many times each shift, the worker soon becomes very competent at completing the task.

There are disadvantages to flow production, however. It requires large amounts of capital equipment in order to work. This equipment is set up to make a particular product, such as a model of car. If the business decides to change the product, it can be very difficult, if not impossible, to make the changes. This, and the fact that very large numbers of products need to be made to keep costs down, keep it out of the reach of small businesses. Another issue is that working on a flow production line can become repetitive. Workers can get bored doing the same thing many times a day. Mistakes can result, meaning the business must keep a careful watch on quality at each stage of production.

Flow production

And more

Mass production was made popular by Henry Ford more than 100 years ago. Ford moved car making away from craft production, when a small number of cars were made at the same time, to mass production. The idea was not new even then. The benefits of having workers specialise in one part of the production process had been known for years. Adam Smith, an early economist, had written about the advantages of division of labour and specialisation in 1776.

Mass production is far more capital intensive than **labour intensive**. By capital, we mean buildings, machinery and equipment. With craft production it is the skill of the worker that is most valued, but mass production values capital more. The whole assembly line is designed to make it as simple as possible for workers to make their contribution to the process. Jobs have been deskilled, so anyone could perform the tasks with the minimum of training. It is said that it is the skill of the engineers who set up the mass production system that matters, rather than the workers who operate it.

Automation helps keep down labour costs. Many mass production processes use robots, which are able to perform repetitive jobs without a break. Robots are expensive to buy and install, but once they are set up they only have energy and maintenance costs. Robots also have the advantage of being able to undertake jobs that would be regarded as having a health and safety concern for human operators. Spray painting cars would be an example of this.

Mass production has enabled standardised products to be manufactured much faster than using traditional craft methods. The amount having to be spent on capital and energy is far higher, but with output being so much greater, the cost of making each item falls. This effect of unit costs falling as output increases is known as an economy of scale.

Not all products are suitable for mass production, even if they are able to be standardised. It would be no good going to the expense of setting up an expensive assembly line if it was felt that the item being manufactured would have only a short product life cycle. Assembly lines are difficult to convert to making a different product, so the manufacturer needs to be confident that demand will be strong enough to justify the expenditure. The risk of the product not succeeding in the marketplace, therefore, needs to be minimised if this method of production is to be used.

Even with reduced labour and other costs, UK businesses might find it difficult to compete with foreign manufacturers, such as China. Competition from emerging countries often have untapped sources of raw materials. There are also fewer restrictions on manufacturing. The laws on health and safety and the environmental impact of business are far less regulated in these countries.

Mass production

Did you know...

Adam Smith's portrait appears on the back of £20 notes. There is also an illustration of division of labour on the banknote.

Have a go!

Group activities

Design a building, or something similar, that could be made using children's Lego bricks. Break down the construction into a series of tasks needed to produce the item. Draw a flow chart to show these different stages. Use this flow chart to lay out your classroom to become a Lego building factory. You will need to make sure you have enough of the right-sized bricks at each production stage. Now start production, with one person at each stage. Time how long it takes to produce each item when production gets started. Compare this time with how long it takes for one person to make the item from start to finish.

Discussion

Discuss what issues a business faces if it decides to move from labour-intensive to capital-intensive methods of production.

Web-based activity

Produce a series of information sheets on the stages involved in making Ben & Jerry's ice cream. Use the Ben & Jerry's website to help you with this assignment. Display the information sheets in the classroom to show the processes involved in making ice cream in large quantities.

Quickfire questions

1   In which year was Ben & Jerry's set up?
2   Why is the ice-cream mix heated in the production process?
3   What is the function of a variegator in ice-cream production?
4   Most of Ben & Jerry's ice cream is sold in what size carton?
5   What is flow production?
6   Give an example of deskilling.
7   What is meant by capital-intensive production?
8   Explain two disadvantages of flow production from the employee's point of view.
9   Explain two advantages of using robots in the production process over human labour.
10 Explain why emerging economies, such as China, are able to produce products cheaper than UK companies.

Hit the spot

> Describe what is meant by flow production.

>> Explain two advantages of using flow production to manufacture goods.

>>> Discuss whether flow production is the best way to manufacture products.

Cracking the code

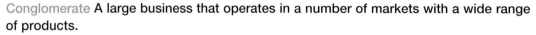

Conglomerate A large business that operates in a number of markets with a wide range of products.

Economies of scale The reasons why costs per item fall as more output is made.

Automation Machinery that can control itself when running without human intervention.

Flow production Products made continuously along an assembly line, with something being added at each stage.

Division of labour Having workers become specialists at one part of the production process.

Labour intensive Requiring a large number of workers compared with the amount of capital used. The opposite of capital intensive.

Chapter 23
Efficiency and lean production

IN THE NEWS

Toyota

Toyota Motor Corporation is a Japanese multinational manufacturer that has been operating since the 1930s. The company has manufacturing bases in several countries spread throughout the world. It is the world's largest car maker in terms of the number of cars made. The company has shares in other car makers, for instance, it owns half of Daihatsu, and has many subsidiary businesses. Toyota produces a range of products in addition to cars. It makes weaving looms, electric sewing machines and robots used in assembly lines, among many other items.

Toyota has been a key company in developing a completely different way of looking at manufacturing. The company calls this system the Toyota Way. One aspect of the Toyota Way is building a culture of stopping to fix problems before they develop. At one time, if an employee stopped the assembly line in a traditional UK factory, he or she would be disciplined. The view then was that by stopping production, output was lost and, therefore, revenue. Only senior managers were given the authority to halt production in this way. Toyota takes a different view. It believes that it is the duty of any employee to stop production if he or she feels that there is a problem with the quality of the product. By recognising the problem early, it avoids inferior-quality goods being made and having to be scrapped. Toyota believes that empowering employees to make important decisions like this motivates them and keeps them loyal to the business.

Toyota treats problem solving as an important

skill for all employees to have. When errors are discovered, they are made clear to all who are affected by them. Identifying and being open about production problems allows the organisation to learn from its mistakes. The company's view is that a problem that is hidden can easily be ignored and repeated.

Having a well-trained workforce is important for Toyota. Only by investing time and money in employees, the company says, can the business grow. Toyota also tries to standardise tasks as much as possible so that employees become good at doing these jobs. By having many tasks the same, it builds familiarity and avoids mistakes being made.

Toyota also believes in working alongside its suppliers to allow them to improve. By forming close relationship with suppliers, they are more likely to support Toyota in its quest to maintain high standards. They do this by ensuring that supplies are themselves of good quality and are delivered on time.

Take a look at the Toyota website at
www.toyota.co.uk

Standardisation

Toyota, along with other car manufacturers, makes cars in a far different way than when car manufacturing started. In the early days, cars were effectively hand built, using highly skilled workers, a process known as craft production. A result of this was that each product was unique. But while the cars were of high quality and designed to last the owner's lifetime, spare parts often had to be hand built, which made them expensive and hard to come by. Later car manufacturers recognised the problems associated with this and set about standardising spare parts. By doing this, the parts could be used on a range of car models and were far more economical to produce.

Cell production

Cell production

Many manufacturers choose to use flow production to manufacture their products. This is mainly as a result of the benefits identified in the last chapter. You may remember, though, that flow production can have disadvantages. Much of the work has been deskilled and made repetitive and can be completed without too much thought by the worker. Employees also might find themselves working in isolation from everyone else in the factory. As a result of these issues, employees can become bored and there is a temptation to not do as good a job as they should. To overcome the problem of employee

motivation, some companies have turned to another system of manufacturing, cell production.

With cell production, products are manufactured in separate areas within the factory. Each of these areas will have a responsibility for a different part of the manufacturing process. So, in the case of cars, one section, or cell, would produce the bodywork, another would be responsible for the electrical wiring, another would add the engine and so on. Each cell would have its own group of workers, with a job that was big enough for them to have to use a range of skills. Once a job had been completed, the vehicle is moved to the next cell for another job to be done.

Cell production can lead to efficiency improvements due to increased motivation. Employees often find the experience of working in a team and being given responsibility to complete a large job rewarding.

The production method used to make a product will depend upon several factors. If the demand for a product is very high and the item is standardised, it will probably be cost effective to use flow production. This method allows for the greatest division of labour and economies of scale to be obtained.

Many UK businesses have been influenced by Japanese production processes. Japanese manufacturing developed rapidly during and after the 1950s, long after the UK and the US had industrialised. Japanese businesses studied UK and US companies to see how they could improve on the methods that these countries used. Many of these techniques are known as lean production.

Manufacturing in Japan

Summary

● Toyota has been a key business in changing the way that manufacturing is undertaken
● Employees are empowered under the Toyota method to take more responsibility for improving the production process
● Cell production is a way of eliminating some of the problems caused by flow production

Core knowledge

Lean production

Lean production techniques share an objective – to get as much output (or products) as possible from a fixed amount of inputs (or raw materials and labour). This involves looking at ways to increase the amount that each employee produces, called **labour productivity**, and at methods to reduce the amount of waste produced.

Lean production came about because of the problems associated with mass production. There are good reasons for producing items in bulk:

● cost savings can be made, called economies of scale;
● division of labour allows workers to specialise and become expert and more efficient at their particular jobs;
● there are opportunities to use machinery and automation that reduce the need for labour-intensive methods of production.

Of course, mass production requires a high demand for the product. Many of the products will need to be sold overseas as local markets can become saturated. But we have seen that there are problems with producing in bulk. Work can become limited and repetitive for employees, who can feel that their contribution is small and not valued. As a result, employees become less conscientious in what they do and efficiency falls.

One of the first attempts to create lean production was used by Henry Ford when producing his Model T car. Ford recognised that production costs could be minimised by standardising components as much as possible. Different versions of the Model T were made. Some had different styles of bodywork, some were convertibles and others were more like trucks to be used as delivery vans. But Ford used as many standardised components as possible on these different versions to keep costs down. This even went as far as the range of colours available. Ford once joked: a customer can have a car painted any colour that he wants so long as it is black. Setting up paint shops to use only one colour helped to reduce production costs. Equipment would not have to be cleaned when a new colour was introduced, which saved the company time and money. Black paint was chosen because it dried quicker than other colours, which was another cost saving.

And more

There are many aspects to lean production. Here are just three of them. While each is different, they share the same approach of attempting to improve efficiency and by so doing bringing down production costs.

- *Just in time (JIT)*. JIT involves not having large amounts of raw materials in stock but having only enough for a company's immediate needs. This saves money for the business in several ways. There is no need for a warehouse where materials are held or the staff to look after it. When stock arrives at the factory, it is delivered straight to where it will be used. There is a risk involved with JIT, however. JIT relies on sophisticated computer systems to ensure that the quantities of stock ordered and delivered are correct. Stock is ordered only as and when it is needed; there is no scope for having stockpiles. This process needs to be carried out very accurately or production could come to a standstill.

- *Quality circles*. With quality circles, employees are encouraged to meet and discuss ways in which production could improve. It is assumed that those who are actually making the products are in the best position to see how improvements could be made. There is another benefit of these meetings: employees get a wider view of what is happening within the business. The workers are more likely to understand how their own actions affect other parts of the factory, so they will be more inclined to have a wider view of production.

- *Kaizen*. Kaizen is a Japanese expression that translates into continuous improvement. When a kaizen approach to work is followed, employees are empowered to look for ways in which the production process can be improved upon. Kaizen assumes that production is never perfect; there is always something which can be performed better. Even the smallest improvement, it is argued, can cause huge cost savings in the long run. Many small changes can lead to overall increases in productivity. For example, an employee might suggest that rather than reaching down for a spanner to tighten a nut, it is placed in a holder near his or her hand. This might save just two seconds each time the spanner is used. But if the tool is used 100 times a shift, then the saving is more than three minutes. If there are nine other employees using similar tools, the time saving is 30 minutes. For three shifts a day, the saving becomes about 475 hours a year, which is about 12 weeks' work for one person.

Taking a kaizen
approach: moving the
spanner

Did you know...

The first type of car to be made using mass-production methods was the Ford Model T, which sold 15 million vehicles.

Have a go!

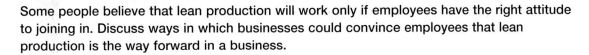

Group activity

Visit a fast-food restaurant or draw on your memory of previous visits. These places often use very efficient ways to produce and then serve you with the food that you buy. Give some examples of where you think lean production techniques have been used. Suggest ways in which the efficiency of these restaurants can be improved even further.

Discussion

Some people believe that lean production will work only if employees have the right attitude to joining in. Discuss ways in which businesses could convince employees that lean production is the way forward in a business.

Web-based activity

Find examples of ways in which real businesses use lean production techniques.

Quickfire questions

1 Besides cars, what else does Toyota make?
2 When would a Toyota employee stop the production line from running?
3 Why did Toyoda become Toyota?
4 Kaizen is a Japanese term: what does it mean?
5 How did Ford save money by making only black Model T cars?
6 What is meant by standardisation?
7 What do the initials JIT stand for?
8 Outline two disadvantages of flow production to employees.
9 Give two ways in which cell production differs from flow production.
10 Give two advantages to a business of operating quality circles.

Hit the spot

> Describe what is meant by lean production.

>> Explain two ways in which just in time can result in lower costs for a business.

>>> Discuss which production method has the lowest costs: cell production or flow production.

Cracking the code

Subsidiary businesses Businesses often known by their own names but which are owned by a parent company.

Standardisation A system of using identical parts or ways of making products, in order to reduce production costs.

Labour productivity A measure of how much each worker produces. If 10 employees produce 150 items a day, their productivity is 150 ÷ 10 = 15 items per worker. The higher the productivity, the more on average each person produces.

Chapter 24
Benefits and challenges of growth

Alliance Boots plc

Chemist business Boots can trace its history back to 1849 when John Boot opened a herbal remedy shop in Nottingham. The business expanded, not just by opening more high-street stores but also by manufacturing pharmaceutical products at its Nottingham factory. After some unsuccessful attempts to diversify into non-healthcare industries, the shareholders agreed to a merger with rival Alliance UniChem in 2006. Alliance UniChem was a European healthcare distribution company that supplied pharmacies and hospitals. The company itself was formed by the merger of UniChem with Alliance Sante in 1997. When Alliance Unichem merged with Boots to create Alliance Boots, the business owned more than 1000 of its own pharmacies.

The creation of Alliance Boots allowed both merging companies to save on their costs. It was estimated that by merging, the cost savings would be more than £100 million each year. When cost savings occur as the size of a business increases, it is known as benefiting from economies of scale.

Two large companies cannot just decide to go ahead and merge. They may need to seek permission from the government. There may be reasons why the government is unhappy about the merger and can decide to stop it from happening, or impose restrictions on the arrangement. In the case of Alliance Boots, the government was worried that the two businesses both had pharmacies and that there could be a reduction in the amount of competition.

The government was not concerned too much about the amount of competition nationally in the pharmacy business but it did express concerns about local competition. It would not make commercial sense for the new merged company to operate two pharmacies that were close together. The government identified 38 places where the merger would result in one pharmacy closing because another Alliance Boots chemist existed within a mile. There were another 61 locations where there were three competing pharmacies, which would be reduced to two. Yet despite these reservations, the government allowed the merger to go ahead.

@ Take a look at the Alliance Boots website at **www.allianceboots.com**

The same amount of milk: which is cheaper?

Economies of scale

The main reason why businesses merge is to help them reduce their costs. When a business doubles in size but costs go up by less than double, we say there are economies of scale. These economies of scale come about for several reasons.

Bulk-buying economies

These are sometimes called purchasing economies. You are probably aware that, if you buy large quantities of a product, you tend to get a better deal than by buying in smaller volumes. A large packet of cornflakes is cheaper per serving than the same-size portion from a small packet. It is the same in business. Suppliers will usually give a discount if large amounts are bought. They do this because the suppliers themselves find it relatively cheaper to deal in large amounts. It will probably cost the supplier the same for the paperwork and delivery van to supply an office with 500 reams of stationery as it does for an order of 50 reams. This cost saving can be passed on to the customer. Also suppliers offer reductions on big orders to encourage these customers to remain with them.

Financial economies

Small businesses can find it hard to obtain finance and when they do obtain it, the cost of the finance is often quite high. This is because small businesses are seen as being riskier than larger businesses that have developed a good track record. Banks and other financial institutions feel more confident about lending funds to larger businesses, as the risk of the loan not being repaid is lower. As a result, the banks are often willing to lend at a lower rate of interest.

Technical economies

Larger businesses will make more efficient use of existing machinery. A machine that is used for only a few hours a day might be running far longer when the business expands. If the machine costs £200 a week to lease, it is far more cost effective to have it running for longer. Large businesses can justify using more advanced machinery, possibly that which is automated and lowers labour costs. As the business grows, it may be worth considering mass production techniques, which are a more efficient form of production. A larger business can also afford to invest more in research and development.

Managerial economies

As a business grows, there is greater potential for the managers to specialise in particular tasks. Rather than having a general manager who takes on all roles, specialists can be hired. There may be a human resource manager, a sales and marketing manager and a finance manager. Specialist managers are likely to be more efficient as they are more experienced and qualified at performing these particular roles compared with a general manager in a smaller firm trying to perform all of the jobs.

Summary

- A merger occurs when two businesses agree to join together to become a single organisation
- Many businesses merge to save costs and to become more profitable
- Economies of scale is the term used to describe the ways in which the cost per item produced falls as a business gets bigger

Did you know...

Merger negotiations are often conducted with great secrecy because the two businesses do not want their share prices to be affected by the talks. Share prices can be used to work out how much each business is worth.

Core knowledge

Mergers are a good way for a business to expand rapidly and achieve cost savings that can help it improve its profitability. There is another advantage too: if the two companies are in the same business, the merger takes out a competitor. A merger between two similar businesses is known as horizontal integration.

Governments are particularly concerned about horizontal mergers. The reduction in competition can have an effect on consumers. Less competition tends to reduce the quality of the service and to raise prices. If the government feels that a potential merger is not in the public interest, it has the power to block it. This is not something that a government will do without careful research. Sometimes a merger might be the only way that two businesses can remain profitable. Without it, they may both go under, with many job losses, something the government would not want to happen.

It is also possible that the cost savings made by merging businesses might be passed on to customers as lower prices. Because it has made cost savings, the new business can afford to lower its prices yet maintain its former profit levels. It is never entirely clear whether a merger will result in lower or higher prices – both are possibilities.

Did you know...

When two businesses merge, it is usual for both companies to keep their separate identities. This is because they often have strong brands that could suffer with a name change.

And more

When businesses become larger, it doesn't necessarily mean that there will be cost savings. Growing businesses bring with them several challenges that could actually cause costs to rise rather than fall. We call these factors diseconomies of scale. If output doubles and costs rise by more than twice, then diseconomies of scale have taken place. Possible reasons for diseconomies include the following:

- *The divorce of ownership from control.* In a small organisation, the owners of the business will probably be the people who manage it. So the owners and controllers are the same people and there will be no conflict of interests. The owners will direct or manage the business so their own personal objectives are achieved. As businesses grow, we have already seen that specialist managers are recruited. These managers may not have the same objectives as the owners, the shareholders. Managers might be more concerned with making themselves look important by employing more staff than are really needed or by having an expensive company car. Such things would reduce the business's profitability, which could be what the shareholders expect from the business.

- *Communications and co-ordinating activities.* Large businesses can bring with them communication problems. Businesses that have become large and complex will very likely have an organisation chart that contains several layers. We read in a previous chapter about difficulties that can arise from having a top-down approach where messages and ideas need to move from layer to layer until they reach the people at the bottom of the hierarchy. This can be a particular issue if the business is based in more than one location. Businesses can tackle this problem by decentralising and delegating authority to each site. However, this could result in losing the benefits of some economies of scale. Having to duplicate managers and other resources at each location, for instance, could undo the potential cost savings. The same is true when it comes to managers co-ordinating business activities. It is much easier for managers to keep an eye on projects, making adjustments as required, when everyone involved is in a single location. Overseeing activities over a range of locations and employees can be far more difficult to co-ordinate. As a result, costs could rise once again.

- *Demotivation and alienation of staff.* Many large businesses undertake some aspect of mass production. We have already seen that specialisation, or the division of labour, can make work dull and repetitive. This can, in turn, lead to employees being switched off and demotivated, leading to sloppy work and increased wastage of materials. Working in a large business where you are responsible for only a small part of the process can make employees wonder whether their contribution really matters. Consequently they can lose heart, resulting in an increased number of mistakes.

- *The optimal size of a business.* Some economists and business experts believe that there is actually an ideal size for a business, which they call the optimum level of output. This is the point at which a business's economies and diseconomies of scale balance each other out. This would be the output where the cost of making each item is at its lowest. If businesses increase output beyond this point, costs rise. If output is below the optimum, then costs could be cut by raising the amount produced. This theory assumes that everything remains the same, which is unlikely in reality. We saw earlier in the book that companies that use Japanese-style lean production methods could overcome some of the problems encountered by growing businesses.

Have a go!

Group activity

Produce a PowerPoint presentation or a podcast, explaining how businesses can reduce costs for each of the economies of scale mentioned in this book.

Web-based activity

Purchasing economies of scale are the discounts that businesses get by buying large quantities. Research the price of sports clothing or footwear on the internet to discover how big a discount can be achieved by buying in bulk. You will need to search for a wholesaler for the product that interests you.

Discussion

Managers of large companies are sometimes accused of not worrying too much about what the owners, the shareholders, want from the business. Very likely shareholders are looking for high profits so that they receive a good dividend and the value of their shares will rise. Discuss ways in which managers of large businesses could be held more accountable to what the shareholders want.

Quickfire questions

1 In which city did Boots first open a shop?
2 In which year did Boots merge with Alliance UniChem?
3 What is the most important reason why businesses merge?
4 Give another name for bulk-buying economies of scale.
5 What is the name of the economy of scale gained by using machinery for more hours each week?
6 What is a horizontal merger?
7 Outline what is meant by the optimum size of a business.
8 Explain why many merged businesses keep their own separate identities.
9 Explain how flow production can result in diseconomies of scale.
10 Explain what is meant by the divorce of ownership from control.

Hit the spot

> Describe what is meant by an economy of scale.

>> Explain two reasons why the government might not allow two businesses to merge.

>>> Discuss whether businesses will always benefit from growing bigger.

Cracking the code

Pharmaceutical **To do with the medicine and drugs industry.**

Merger **Two or more businesses joining together and operating as a single organisation.**

Chapter 25
Maintaining quality assurance in growing businesses

IN THE NEWS

British Standards Institution (BSI)

The BSI Group was founded as the Engineering Standards Committee in London in 1901 and became known as the British Standards Institution in 1921. The organisation produces and publishes standards which are sold to other businesses. What this means is BSI, along with a committee of volunteers, looks at the way products should perform and sets the standard for the quality of the finished product. BSI and the technical committee decide what the minimum standard should be for a product or service, which BSI then publishes. These standards are sold to other businesses to cover the costs involved. When a business makes a product that meets the minimum standards and has been independently tested by BSI, it is allowed to place the Kitemark on the item. This shows potential buyers that the product meets the published standard, and also the Kitemark scheme rules. Many businesses choose to make their products to BSI and Kitemark standards as customers want reassurance that the products they buy are up to scratch.

So, what exactly is a standard? A standard is an agreed set of requirements for a product or a repeatable way of producing a product or providing a service. It is a description of the quality of a product and how this quality is achieved in practice. This detailed information is then produced in a document that is called the standard.

Standards are created by drawing on the experience and expertise of producers, sellers, buyers and users. A group of experts will meet and decide what standard is needed for a particular product. For example, BSI would talk to the manufacturers and users of industrial safety boots. Between them they would agree what the minimum standards should be for this type of footwear. They would agree how high and heavy a weight could be dropped on to the boot without damaging the wearer's feet. They would also agree how long it would take acid and other dangerous materials to seep into the boot. Having set this standard, manufacturers of safety boots would have to make sure their boots passed the tests in order to be compliant with the standard.

Standards help to make life simpler for consumers and for businesses as the requirements for and quality of the product are established by an independent organisation. This saves companies having to spend large amounts of money on research and product marketing. Marking the product with the number of the standard, e.g. BS 1234, also sends a message to consumers: this product reaches a recognised standard, which increases their confidence in the item.

 Take a look at the BSI website at **www.bsigroup.com** or visit **www.Kitemark.com**

Did you know...

BSI created one of the world's first and longest-lasting quality marks in 1903, when the letters 'B' and 'S' (for British Standards) were combined to produce the Kitemark logo.

By law, some products have to conform to national or European standards before they can legally be sold in this country. Motorcycle helmets are an example of this. Those businesses not required to possess a standard may still choose to use one. There are several reasons for doing this.

Standards are not just about the quality of the final product. They are also used to ensure that working practices are efficient and improve productivity. If a business looks at the way it makes goods or provides a service, it could gain a competitive advantage over other businesses by improving its efficiency and effectiveness. Improved efficiency mean that costs are lowered, which can result in extra profits and becoming the key player in an industry. Increases in market leadership can allow a business to take a leading role in shaping the industry in which it operates.

Standards can be used to improve the quality of communications within an organisation. If a business can demonstrate good links with its suppliers, it can be given an award for this. This would also apply to the system of communications within the business, whereby all employees are kept informed about what is happening in the company.

Standards allow a company to attract customers by assuring them that the product it sells is of good quality. Operating to a recognisable and trusted standard makes the product stand out from competitors. This is particularly important as consumers become increasingly informed about the choices available to them. An example of this is consumers' growing concern for environmental matters. There are standards available to businesses to reassure customers that they are conforming to recognised procedures when it comes to acting responsibly towards the environment. This would include attempting to reduce the business's carbon footprint and ensuring that all waste material is recycled rather than being sent to landfill sites.

There is often a mistaken belief that all businesses should produce goods to the highest possible standards. If this was to happen, the manufacturing costs would be far higher and, as a result, prices would more than likely have to increase. Consumers would clearly not be happy with rising prices. Most are willing to accept 'good enough' quality within the products that they buy. This means the quality of the product must be at least as good as the consumer expects. A customer will not expect a coat to last half a lifetime, as people did 100 years ago. Fashion changes mean people want to change the style they wear regularly. Therefore, there is little point in manufacturers spending a lot making clothes durable when consumers do not really want this. The opposite will be true as well. Even if people buy low-priced goods from budget stores, they expect that certain standards are maintained.

At one time it was considered the responsibility of the purchaser to check that the quality was good enough before the item was bought. This requirement was known by the Latin legal expression **caveat emptor**, which translates to 'let the buyer beware'.

Did you know...

In 2008, BSI was recognised as a UK Business Superbrand. This was the fourth year in a row it was acknowledged with the award. Kitemark is also a Business Superbrand in its own right. The word Kitemark and the Kitemark logo are registered trademarks of BSI.

Summary

- BSI is an organisation that sets agreed standards for the quality of a range of products and services
- By law some safety equipment must conform to a British or European standard before it can legally be sold in the UK
- Businesses can gain a competitive edge by being able to state to customers that their product reaches a BSI standard and has a Kitemark
- Conforming to production standards can improve a business's efficiency

Did you know...

BSI has produced over 30,000 standards and publications that businesses and government bodies can access and use.

Core knowledge

Quality is much easier to maintain in a small business than it is in larger organisations. The owners of small businesses are more likely to know first hand what is happening in their organisation and can respond quickly when sales suffer because quality is falling. As a business grows, however, communications within the organisation can become more difficult, resulting in deterioration in quality. There are also effects of mass production that we looked at in an earlier chapter. Repetitive, low-skilled work can make the work boring, which can lead to errors being made.

Quality assurance

Larger businesses often adopt a system of quality assurance (QA) to maintain quality within the business. A set of activities or procedures is created to ensure that products satisfy customer requirements. No system of quality assurance can guarantee that the quality will always reach minimum standards, but by having procedures in place it makes it less likely that faulty goods will get through to the customer.

Two principles that many businesses use when creating a QA system are:

- fit for purpose – the product should be up to its intended use;
- right first time – avoids having to re-do things, causing waste, by making sure no errors happen.

Both of these principles try to avoid discovering mistakes after the product has been made, as this can be very costly. Even worse are customers discovering the mistakes, which can lead to the business getting a poor reputation. To avoid these errors, a business will probably have QA procedures for checking that production systems are operating as they should be and that areas such as communications both within the company and with suppliers and customers function properly.

Under TQM (see below), everyone on the production line is responsible for quality

Testing product quality

And more

Total Quality Management (TQM) is a quality assurance method. What is different about this method is that rather than leave quality in the hands of company inspectors, everyone within the organisation is meant to have responsibility for quality. This system is used by Toyota, which was studied in an earlier chapter.

The principle of TQM lies in making the maintenance of quality second nature to those who work in the company. It is not seen as something that needs to be looked at occasionally as production takes place, but should be at the forefront of everyone's thinking. An office worker would not walk past a machine that was malfunctioning – he or she would be expected to stop the machine or sort the problem out if possible, even if that was not his or her job.

An argument in favour of TQM, besides the improvement in quality, is that it motivates staff. Many people respond well to being given responsibility and they become more enthusiastic as a result. Others might argue that not everyone is looking for this level of responsibility and many prefer to get on with doing their job, letting others worry about the quality.

Have a go!

Group activity

Produce a set of standards tests for a portion of fries from a fast-food outlet, or another product. Meet as a group and agree upon what you regard as the basic standards for this product. You might want to decide upon the weight of the portion, the width of the individual fries, their length and how crispy they are. You will need to devise tests to see whether your sample passes. This could include a bending test to see how far the fry bends before breaking. When you have agreed the standard, buy some fries and test them. Produce a league table of which outlets' fries pass the test. Write a report on your findings.

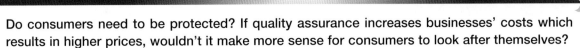

Discussion

Do consumers need to be protected? If quality assurance increases businesses' costs which results in higher prices, wouldn't it make more sense for consumers to look after themselves?

Web-based activity

Research the standards that apply to cycle helmets. You should be able to access this information at sites such as www.cyclehelmets.org. Produce a poster to summarise your findings.

Quickfire questions

1 What do the initials BSI stand for?
2 What does the organisation BSI do?
3 What is a Kitemark?
4 Describe what is meant by a standard.
5 Give an example of a good that is fit for purpose.
6 What do the initials TQM stand for?
7 What is another expression for 'let the buyer beware'?
8 Explain why some products by law must have passed a standard.
9 Explain possible reasons why businesses do not always produce products at the highest quality.
10 Explain why a business that has been awarded a Kitemark would have an advantage over a competitor that has not.

Hit the spot

> What is meant by quality assurance?

>> Explain why it might be more difficult to maintain quality in large businesses than in smaller ones.

>>> Discuss whether the system of TQM would work in all businesses.

Cracking the code

Research and development Often a department within a large business, which is responsible for finding ways of improving products and production, and for putting these ideas into practice.

Caveat emptor The name of an old law that makes the buyer responsible for checking the quality of the product.

Preparing for the controlled assessment

What is a controlled assessment?

Controlled assessments have replaced coursework across all awarding bodies, including AQA. Unlike coursework, there are some restrictions (or controls) which your teacher has to ensure are in place while you do the work.

Your hard work on this GCSE course will be assessed by a combination of exams and controlled assessments.

Why is the controlled assessment needed?

The one-hour exam paper that you sit for each unit of study cannot assess all of the assessment objectives thoroughly.

The controlled assessment gives you the time to show the examiner just how good you are at using business ideas, when you have more time to think carefully about the issues. In the past this was done using coursework, but schools found that coursework took too long to produce, taking away valuable learning time. The controlled assessment was designed to take less time.

Which assessments do I need to do?

The assessments you do will depend on the course you are taking.

- A **short GCSE** business studies course (your school may call this a **half-GCSE**): you have to take a controlled assessment and one exam.

- The **full GCSE** course: two exam papers and a controlled assessment.

- The **double award GCSE** in Applied Business: you do not need to study this unit, but remember you will have other assessments to do later.

The controlled assessment is a significant part of your GCSE. Your final GCSE grade will be greatly influenced by how well you do in this assessment. The Unit 3 controlled assessment makes up 25% of the final grade for the full course GCSE.

The Unit 3 controlled assessment

The controlled assessment for the **full course GCSE** is called Unit 3: Investigating businesses. (Remember that, if you are taking the short course or the double award, you will take a different assessment, not this one.)

'Investigating businesses' is a very general title. Before you start your course, the awarding body, AQA, will set a more specific task that you will need to complete under controlled conditions – the controlled assessment. It will include some background information relating to the topics you learn about during the course.

The task changes each year. This means if you need to re-sit the controlled assessment, you will be tackling a different task the second time.

AQA publish details of the latest controlled assessment each year: they send the details to teachers and publish them on the web notice board for Business Studies.

Table of assessments for the different courses: who does what
Note: Each exam mentioned here lasts one hour.

	Exam: Setting up a business (Unit 13)*	Exam: Setting up a business (Unit 1)	Controlled assessment: Investigating small businesses (Unit 14)	Exam: Growing as a business (Unit 2)	Controlled assessment: Investigating businesses (Unit 3)	Other assessments
Short course GCSE	✓		✓			
Full course GCSE		✓		✓	✓	
Double-award GCSE		✓				✓

* Unit 13 covers the same material as Unit 1. However, the Unit 13 exam paper will have different questions to the Unit 1 paper.

Carrying out the assessment

Your teacher will give you information about the controlled assessment task when he or she feels the time is right.

If you would like to research more about this assessment, then you will find plenty of information on the AQA website, www.aqa.org.uk. The fastest way to find the information is to do a search on the site for 'GCSE business studies controlled assessment 2012' (if you are taking your exams and controlled assessment in 2012).

There are two stages to the controlled assessment:

● Planning and researching the topics covered in the assignment.

● Writing up the assignment.

Planning and research

You teacher should only set you off on the assignment once you have been taught the material that it covers. For example, if the assignment scenario deals with marketing, then you need to be familiar with the marketing section of both books before you start to work. Your assignment research should relate to the particular details of the assignment, not the basic terms.

During the planning stage, you will be allowed to work with other students, if your teacher thinks that this is suitable for you and your class. (The next stage, writing up, is done under test conditions.)

You are advised by AQA to spend between five and eight hours preparing for the task. During this time you are expected to be able to:

● Select relevant information from a variety of sources.

● Explain what you have discovered in your research, and **why** you chose to do the research in the way that you did. For instance, if the scenario is about an entrepreneur thinking about starting a small service sector business, you may be required to conduct some market research into the service to be provided.

● Consider the methods that would be suitable for that type of business, and conduct the market research yourself.

● Support your choice of method when you write up the assessment, as well as outlining your actual findings.

- Explore any issues that have been raised in your research. For example, if a business has a choice between two options, such as lowering its prices to attract customers, or advertising more instead, you will have to put forward clear points for and against both options in order to score well.

Keep careful notes of all your findings during this stage of the assessment, as these notes can be used when you write up.

You are allowed to ask for help from your teacher at this stage in the assessment. He or she may, for instance, get you to look at alternative ways of thinking about the topic or solving the problem. Your teacher may also advise you on sources of information, maybe by suggesting a website to visit. Your teacher, however, has to let AQA know exactly what type of assistance has been given to you.

Writing up the assignment

You will have about three hours to write up your assignment. This time is not fixed; it is just a recommendation from AQA. You are allowed more time, but it shouldn't be necessary. Extra time is available if you have special educational needs, and this will be explained to you by your school.

AQA is not looking for very long and rambling answers. It is possible to score high marks with brief pieces of work that get straight to the point and show your skills of application, analysis and evaluation.

Your teacher will probably run the writing-up time in more than one session, probably during normal timetabled lessons. If there is more than one session, you will not be allowed to take any of your notes or your written work out of the room between sessions. This material must be collected by your teacher and kept safe until the next session.

During the writing time, you will need to complete the task that has been set by AQA. This may take the form of a report, or some other style of presenting your findings. You may be able to produce your account on a computer, but hand-written responses are just as good.

You will need to sign a declaration when you hand in your assignment to say that your assessment is your own work

How is the assessment marked?

Your teacher will give your work a mark out of 40. Teachers will be looking for three skills, called Assessment Objectives (see table).

The teacher will also assess your ability to write good quality English and present clear arguments. This is known as the quality of written communication (QWC). Writing with few spelling or other mistakes will be rewarded. You will also score well on QWC if you are able to use business terms as you write.

Once your work has been marked by your teacher, AQA will ask for a sample of the work or, in some cases, all the students' work to be sent away. This is simply to check that everyone's work has been marked to the same standard, whichever school they are at.

Assessment objective (AO)	Maximum marks
AO1: having knowledge and understanding of business ideas and terms	12 marks
AO2: being able to apply, or use, these business ideas and terms to explain the issues in your assignment	14 marks
AO3: showing evidence that you have brought in business ideas to explore the information that you have collected. You also need to make judgements on how useful this evidence is.	14 marks

Appendix: International Financial Reporting Standards

A European Union regulation of 2005 says that financial statements must use International Financial Reporting Standards (IFRS). You may therefore come across different names for the same things: the old name and the new IFRS name.

Balance sheets

The structure of the balance sheet has not changed.

Old term	IFRS term
Fixed assets	Non-current assets
Stocks	Inventories
Debtors	Trade and other receivables
Creditors	Trade and other payables
Long-term liabilities	Non-current liabilities
Shareholders' funds	Total equity or total shareholders' equity

Reserves now include 'retained earnings', which used to be called 'retained or undistributed profits'.

Profit and loss accounts

The appropriation account is now dealt with separately from income.

Old term	IFRS term
Turnover	Revenue
Stocks	Inventories
Gross profit less expenses	Operating profit

Index

Note: page numbers in **bold** refer to key word definitions.

above-the-line 44, 45, **49**
Accountability Rating 17–18
accountants 59–60
   financial accountants 59–60
   management accountants 59–60
accounts *see* company accounts
acid test ratios 83, 85, **87**
acquisitions 6, **10**
advertising
   job vacancies 100, 101
   promotional 45–7
agents 23–4, **27**, 53
AIDA (Attention, Interest, Desire,
   Action) 46, **49**
alienation 138
Alliance Boots 135–6
Alternative Investment Market
   (AIM) 11, **16**
annual accounts 13, **16**, 59
annual general meeting (AGM) 15
Apple iPhone 39, 40, 81
appraisals 106, 108, 114
apprentice system 106
appropriation account 68, 69, 70,
   73
Argos 51
Arsenal FC 67
assembly lines 121, 126, 129
Assessment Objectives 148–9
assets 58, 64
   on the balance sheet 75–8, 83
   current 77, 83, **87**
   definition **66, 80**
   fixed 76–7
   intangible 75, **80**
   leasing 62
   liquidity 82
   net 76, 77
   net current 77
   sale of 63
Aston Science Park 22

autocratic management styles 114,
   117
automation 121, 124, 126, **128,** 131

balance sheets 60, 74–80, **80**
   assets 75–8, 83
   capital 75
   current ratios 83
   example 77
   liabilities 74–8, 83
   publication 78
   using 76, 78
   vertical 75, 78
Bank of England base rate 62
bank loans 8, 62, 63–4
banking crisis 74
batch production 124–5
below-the-line 44, 45, **49**
Ben & Jerry's Ice Cream 123–5
BGS *see* British Gas Services
Blackberry Storm 39, 40
Boots the Chemist 135–6
brand image 37, 47
brand names 7, **10**, 37, 137
break even 20
British Gas Services (BGS) 105–6
British Standards Institute (BSI)
   141–3
broadcast media 46, 47
bulk decreasing industries 25, **27**
bulk increasing industries 25, **27**
bulk-buying (purchasing) economies
   136
business aims 3, 17–21
business failure 69
business growth/expansion 2–4,
   5–10
   advantages of 2–3
   benefits and challenges of 135–40
   as business aim/objective 18
   and business organisation 2

   external 31
   through franchising 7, 8
   funding 8
   horizontal 9
   internal 31
   through licensing 7
   and the market 31
   and market sector 20
   and the marketing mix 31–2,
      34–5, 36
   through mergers 5, 6
   through organic growth 6, 8, **10**
   organising 92–7
   overseas 18, 19, 23–4, 25
   overstretching 7, **10**
   price strategies for 40–1
   and quality assurance 141–5
   'staying small' 32
   through takeovers 6
   vertical 9
business location 4, 22–7
   and costs 4, 24
   and factors of production 23
   and international expansion 23–4,
      25
   key questions regarding 23
   and revenue 24
   and span of control 93
   and type of business 23
   see also place (marketing mix)
business objectives 3, 17–21
business organisation 1–27
   business aims and objectives
      17–21
   business growth/expansion 2–4,
      5–10
   business location 22–7
   introduction to 2–4
   legal structures 11–16
business ownership
   and business growth/expansion 7

business ownership – *contd*
  and control 2, 138
  divorce from control 138
business size
  optimal 138
  and pricing strategies 41
  and promotion 45

Cadbury 5–7, 8
capital **80,** 85
  share capital 61, 62, 63
  venture capital 62, **66**
  working capital 75–6, **80**
capital depreciation 75
capital equipment 125, 126
capital intensive production 126
car assembly 125, 129, 132
carbon footprint 19, **21**
'cash calls' 61
cash flow forecasts 60
caveat emptor 142, **145**
cell production 130–1
Center Parcs 11–12
centralisation 95
channels of distribution *see*
    distribution channels
communication
  and diseconomies of scale 138
  and layers of management 94
  and motivation 90–1, 114
  quality of 142
  and span of control 93
Companies Act 1985 59
company accounts 58–60, 78
  annual accounts 13, **16,** 59
  management accounts 59–60
  window dressing 78
  see also profit and loss accounts
competition
  between team members 115
  and mergers 135, 137
competitive advantage 141
competitive markets 106, **110,** 111
competitive pricing 41, 42
competitors 76
  buying shares in 13
conglomerates 123, **128**
control
  and business ownership 2, 138
  divorce from ownership 138

span of 93, **97**
controlled assessment 146–8
  Assessment Objectives 148
  carrying out 147–8
  marking scheme 148
  planning and research 147–8
  Unit 3 146
  writing up 148
corporate hospitality 45, **49**
corporate social responsibility (CSR)
    17, 18, **21**
cost accounting 59
cost of sales 68, **73**
cost-plus pricing 41
costs 70
  and business growth 137, 138
  and business location 4, 24
  direct (fixed) 59
  and distribution 52
  indirect (variable) 59
  and lean production 121–2, 132
  and mergers 135, 137
  of promotion 47
  running 59
  set-up 59
craft production 130
creditors 75, 76, **80**
CSR *see* corporate social
    responsibility
customer assistants 98
customer service 20
customers 91
  choice 51–2

day release 107
debentures 15
debt 78
debtors 76, **80**
decentralisation 95, 138
decision-making 95
deindustrialisation 120
delayering 94
delegated responsibility 93, 138
Dell 51
demand
  and business growth 8
  changes in 34
demergers 5, 9, **10**
democratic management styles 114,
    117

demolition industry 92
demotivation 138
deskilling 126, 130
destroyer pricing 42, **43**
discrimination 101
diseconomies of scale 9, 138
distribution 51–3
  stockless 54
distribution channels 51–3, **55**
  intermediary 51, 53, **55**
  long-chain 51, 53, **55**
  short-channel 51, 53
diversification 18, **21**, 36, **38**
diversify 5, 7, **10**
dividends 13–15, **16,** 62–3, 71, 91
division of labour 125, **128,** 131, 138
downloads 50
Dubai Sports City 44

economies of scale 9, 34, 124, 131,
    135–7
  bulk-buying (purchasing)
      economies 136
  definition **38, 128**
  financial economies 136
  managerial economies 136
  technical economies 136
  see also diseconomies of scale
efficiency 129–34, 141
Egg Banking plc 111–12, 113, 114
employees 106
  alienation 138
  boredom 121, 130
  demotivation 138
  development 114
  empowerment 122
  loyalty 111, 115, **117,** 129
  motivation 111–15
  performance management 106,
      108
  and quality circles 132
  training 99, 105–10, 129
  see also staff development plans;
      staff recruitment
empowerment 122
entrepreneurs
  and business organisation 2
  and venture capital 62
environmental concerns 17–18, 19,
    142

ethical business 3, 18–19, **21,** 124
exports 23, **27**

factors of production 23, **27**
feedback 114
finance departments 58
finance for large businesses 57–87
   balance sheets 74–80
   and business growth/expansion 8
   financial records 58, 59–60
   introduction to 58–60
   long-term 63
   medium-term 63
   profit and loss accounts 67–73
   ratios 81–7
   short-term 63
   sources of 58, 61–6
      external 62, 63
      internal 62–3
      and performance 63–4
financial accountants 59–60
financial economies 136
'fit for purpose' 143
flat hierarchies 94
flexible working patterns 98
floating a company 62, **66**
flow production 125, **128,** 130, 131
Ford, Henry 126, 132
franchisees 8
franchising 7, 8
franchisors 8
FT 100SE (Footsie) 14

'gaps in the market' 8
GCSEs
   double award 146–7
   full 146–7
   short 146–7
Global Cool Foundation, The 17
governments
   assistance 24, 25
   and mergers 135, 137
grants, government 24, 25
greenhouse gases 19
growth/expansion see business
   growth/expansion

Halifax Bank of Scotland (HBOS) 61
hierarchies 94–5, 138
   flat 94

inverted 95
   matrix 95
horizontal integration 137
hygiene factors 113, **117**

induction 107
infrastructure 23, 24, **27**
inputs 6, **10**
interest rates, Bank of England rate
   62
intermediaries 51, 53, **55**
International Financial Reporting
   Standards 149
Internet
   sales 50, 51, 53
   security 113
intranets 114
inverted hierarchies 95
investment 78
investors 76
iPhone 39, 40, 81

Japanese manufacturing 129–31
job descriptions 100
job interviews 98, 99, 101
job satisfaction 114
just-in-time (JIT) production 54, 132

kaizen 132
Kitemark 141, 142

labour
   division of 125, **128,** 131, 138
   standardisation 121
labour intensive production 126, **128**
labour productivity 131, **134**
labour turnover 99, **104**
Leahy, Sir Terry 99
lean production methods 121–2,
   129–34
leasing 62
legal structures 11–16
liabilities 74–8, **80**
   current 83
liability, limited 12
licensing 7
limited companies 78
   see also private limited companies;
      public limited companies
limited liability 12

line managers 93, 94, **97**
   motivation 111–12
liquidity 82, 83, 85
listed (quoted) companies 12
loans 8, 62, 63–4
location see business location; place
   (marketing mix)
logistics 53
long-chain distribution 51, 53, **55**
loss leaders 40, **43**
loyalty, employee 111, 115, **117**

machinery 121, 124, 126, 131
management 76
   and diseconomies of scale 138
   layers of 93–4
   and performance management
      108
   recruitment 98–9, 101
   see also line managers
management accountants 59–60
management accounts 59–60
management style
   autocratic 114, **117**
   democratic 114, **117**
   and motivation 114
managerial economies 136
managing directors 92–4
manufacturing
   and business location 23–5
   and mass production 121
   overseas 126
   standardisation 120–1
   and technological change 120
market dominance 18, **21**
market leaders 18, **21**
market research 31
market sectors/segments
   and business growth/expansion
      20
   and promotion 47
market share
   definition **43**
   as guide to business
      growth/expansion 31
   and pricing strategies 40, 42
marketing 29–55
   direct 46
   introduction 30–2
   marketing mix 33–55

marketing mix 30–1, 33–55
  balance 30–1
  changing 35
  definition **38**
  fluid nature 30–1
  place 30–1, 50–5
  price 30–1, 39–43
  product 30–1, 33–8
  promotion 30–1, 44–9
markets
  and business location 23
  competitive 106, **110,** 111
  gaps in the 8
  mature 33, **38**
  and promotion 46
  size 31
mass production 121, 126, 131
matrix hierarchies 95
mature markets 33, **38**
merchants 53
mergers 5, 6, 135, 137
  definition **10, 140**
  horizontal 137
microbusinesses 32
Million Superheroes Campaign, The
  17
mission statements 19
mobile phones 33–4
  recycling/reusing 17
Monstermob 33–4
mortgages 8
motivation 90–1, 111–17, 130
  and hygiene factors 113
  and remuneration 113
  and Total Quality Management
    144
  see also demotivation
multinationals 129
music industry 50

nationalisation 74
newsletters 114
Northern Rock 74

off-the-job training 107
offshoring 24, 25
on-the-job training 107
operations management 119–45
  benefits and challenges of growth
    135–40

  efficiency 129–34
  introduction 120–2
  lean production 129–34
  production methods 123–8
  quality assurance and growth
    141–5
organic growth 6, 8, **10**
organisation *see* business
  organisation
organisation charts 92–4
organisational culture 114
outsourcing 95
overseas growth/expansion 18, 19,
  23–4, 25
overstretching 7, **10**
ownership *see* business ownership

pay, performance-related 107
penetration pricing 40–1, **43**
people in business 89–117
  appraisals 106, 108
  introduction 90–1
  motivation 90–1, 111–17
  organising growing businesses
    92–7
  staff recruitment 98–104
  training 105–10
performance management
  (appraisals) 106, 108
performance objectives 106
performance-related pay 107
person specifications 100
pharmaceutical products 135, **140**
pharming 113
phishing 113
place (marketing mix) 30–1, 50–5
  and business choice 52
  channels of distribution 51, 52
  and customer choice 51–2
  Internet sales 50, 51, 53
  see also business location
premium pricing 40, **43**
price
  and business size 41
  competitive 41, 42
  cost-plus pricing 41
  and loss leaders 40, **43**
  as part of the marketing mix 30–1,
    39–43
  penetration 40–1, **43**

  predator/destroyer pricing 42, **43**
  premium pricing 40, **43**
  and quality 142
  range 41
  skimming 39, 40, **43**
price makers 42, **43**
price takers 42, **43**
print media 47
private limited companies 3, 11–13
probationary periods 102
product
  actual 37
  augmented 37
  definition **38**
  and growth 34–5, 36
  identity 37
  intangible benefits 36–7
  as part of the marketing mix 30–1,
    33–8
  tangible benefits 36–7
product differentiation 36
product diversification 36, **38**
product endorsement 44, 45
product life cycle 34–5, **38**
  aborted 35
  explosive 35
  extension 35
  revived 35
product mix 36, **38**
product placement 47
product range 36, **38**
production, factors of 23, **27**
production methods 123–8
  batch production 124–5
capital intensive production 126
craft production 130
  flow production 125, **128,** 130, 131
  just-in-time (JIT) production 54,
    132
  labour intensive production 126,
    128
  lean production methods 121–2,
    129–34
  mass production 121, 126, 131
productivity 114
  labour 131, **134**
profit 71
  as business aim/objective 20
  and business growth/expansion 6,
    7, 8

distributed 13, 14, 62
gross 60, 68, 71, **73,** 82
gross profit margin 82, **87**
margins 52, 81–4, **87**
net 60, 69–71, **73,** 82, 85
net profit after taxation 71
net profit margin 82, 83, **87**
quality of 68
ratios 82–3
retained 5, 8, **10,** 13, 62–3, **66,**
    69, 71, **73**
profit and loss accounts 60, 67–73
appropriation account 68, 69, 70,
    73
disadvantages of 71
profit and loss account 68, 69, 70,
    73
trading account 68, 70, **73**
using 69
promotion (marketing mix) 30–1,
    44–9
above-the-line 44, 45, **49**
advertising 45–6
below-the-line 44, 45, **49**
and business size 45
costs 47
coverage 47
and markets 46
penetration 47
promotional strategies 45, **49**
purposes of 45–6
property sector 67
Prudential 111, 112
psychometric tests 102
public limited companies (plcs) 6, 63
annual accounts 59
balance sheets 74
becoming 3, 11–13
definition **10, 16**
profit and loss accounts 67
public relations (PR) 45
public sector businesses 12
pull strategies 51
purchasing economies 136

quality assurance
'fit for purpose' 143
'good enough' quality 142
and growth 141–5
'right first time' 143

quality circles 132
quoted (listed) companies 12

radio advertising 46–7
ratios 60, 81–7
acid test 83, 85, **87**
current 83, 85, **87**
profitability 82–3
Return on Capital Employed 85
raw materials 23
recruitment agencies 102
recycling 17
redundancy 6, **10**
remuneration 113, **117**
research and development 141, **145**
responsibility 144
delegated 93, 138
retailers 52–3
'bricks and clicks' 53
Return on Capital Employed 85
reusing 17
'right first time' 143
rights issues 61, **66**
ringtones 33–4
risk, spreading 7
robots 120, 126
royalties 7, **10**

'sale and leaseback' 64
sales, cost of 68, **73**
sales revenue (turnover) 68, 70, **73**
and business location 24
ratios 82
satnavs 39–40
Schweppes 5, 6
security 62, 63, **66**
share capital 61, 62, 63
shareholders 12–15
and business growth 6, 8–9
and motivation 91
ordinary 14
preference 14
of private limited companies 12,
    13
and takeovers 6
shares 11–15, 58
and business growth 6, 8
and mergers 137
ordinary shares 14
preference shares 14

price 14, 15, 64, 71, 137
of private limited companies 12
rights issues 61, **66**
and takeovers 6
short lists 101
short-channel distribution 51, 53
skimming 39, 40, **43**
small and medium-sized enterprises
    (SMEs) 32
Smith, Adam 126
socialising 114, 115
Solar Aid 17
Southern Demolition Company Ltd
    92–4
span of control 93, **97**
sponsorship 44, 45
staff development plans 108
staff recruitment 98–104
stakeholders 3, 19, 59
standardisation 120–1, 125–6,
    130–2, **134**
standards 141–2
statements 60
stock
and the acid test ratio 83
and just-in-time production 132
Stock Exchange 11, 12, **16,** 63
stockless distribution 54
subordinates 93, **97**
subsidiary businesses 129, **134**
suppliers 91, 129, 136
survival 20

takeovers 6, **10**
targets 106
task complexity 93
taxation 71
teambuilding 115
technical economies 136
technological change 120
Tesco 98–9
Total Quality Management (TQM) 144
Toyota Motor Corporation 129–30,
    131
Toyota Way 129
trading account 68, 70, **73**
training 99, 105–10, 129
day release 107
induction 107
and motivation 91, 114

training – *contd*
  off-the-job 107
  on-the-job 107
turnover *see* sales revenue (turnover)

underwriters 61, 64
Unilever 123

unique selling points (USPs) 46
Unit 3 (controlled assessment) 146

value added 52
venture capital 62, **66**
vision 19
Vodafone 17–19

wholesalers 53
Wilkinson 20
work–life balance 98, **104**
workforce
  diversity 19
  planning 108–9
working capital 75–6, **80**